the THIRD edition

New
Headway

Intermediate
Workbook with key

Liz and John Soars

OXFORD

UNIVERSITY PRESS

OXFORD
UNIVERSITY PRESS

Great Clarendon Street, Oxford OX2 6DP

Oxford University Press is a department of the University of Oxford.
It furthers the University's objective of excellence in research, scholarship,
and education by publishing worldwide in

Oxford New York

Auckland Cape Town Dar es Salaam Hong Kong Karachi
Kuala Lumpur Madrid Melbourne Mexico City Nairobi
New Delhi Shanghai Taipei Toronto

With offices in

Argentina Austria Brazil Chile Czech Republic France Greece
Guatemala Hungary Italy Japan Poland Portugal Singapore
South Korea Switzerland Thailand Turkey Ukraine Vietnam

OXFORD and OXFORD ENGLISH are registered trade marks of
Oxford University Press in the UK and in certain other countries

ISBN-13: 978 0 19 438754 5 International edition

ISBN-13: 978 0 19 439004 0 German edition

Printed and bound in China

ACKNOWLEDGEMENTS

*The authors and publisher are grateful for permission to reproduce the following
copyright material*: p59 'The house is not the same since you left' by Henry
Normal, reprinted by permission of Bloodaxe Books Ltd from Nude
Modelling for the Afterlife (Bloodaxe Books, 1993)

Illustrations by: Martha Gavin pp15, 32; David Hine pp18, 28, 29; Ian Kellas
p61; Joanna Kerr pp35, 79; Barbara McAdams p73; Monotype 9 font catalogue
p16; Harry Venning pp24, 26, 39, 53, 55, 72; Katherine Walker p27, 31, 33, 42,
52, 58, 60, 62, 66, 71, 80; Annabel Wright p59

We would also like to thank the following for permission to reproduce photographs:
Associated Press p5 (E.Thompson); John Birdsall Photography p78; The
Anthony Blake Photo Library p8; Corbis pp 9 (A.Skelly), 13 (J.Horner/grocery),
22 (Bettmann/Helen Keller & Amy Johnson), (Hulton-Deutsch Collection/
Charles Blondin), 25 (J.Hollingsworth/boy), 43 (R.Hellestad/Margaret Atwood),
(Bettmann/Jane Austen), (Bettmann/Marilyn Monroe), (S.I.N./Bob Marley),
(I.Nowinski/David Hockney), (G.Dagli Orti/Vincent Van Gogh), 48 (V.Zwalm/
museum), 51 (M.Beebe), 67 (© Archivo Iconografico, S.A.), 70 (royalty free);
Digital Vision p41; Eyewire p37; Frank Lane Picture Agency p38 (Minden
Pictures/lion cubs); Getty Images pp 6 (S.Derr), 7 (L.Bobbe), 11 (W.Meier), 12
(D.Cody/Vichai), 12 (Aitch/Uma & Sanjit Singh), 13 (P.Chesley/traffic jam), 19
(P.Cade), 20 (Chabruken/John Phillips), 21 (A.Freund), 27 (J.Polillio/Jill and
Jack), 27 (B & M Productions/Sam and Anna), 30 (E.Dreyer/Mr Sanders), 30
(C.Bissell/Ms Maddox), 33 (E.Young), 34 (J.Walker), 38 (A.Wolfe/Masai woman),
39 (M.Junak), 47 (C.Bale), 53 (M.Jefferson/snowboarding), 53 (V.C.L./sailing), 54
(J.William Banagan), 56 (S.Fitchett), 63 (T.Corney/Raoul), 63 (J.Lawrence/Statue
of Liberty), 65 (C.Alpert/Heather), 65 (D.Sacks/Richard), 75 (M.Lewis), 76
(S. Derr); © David Hockney Studio p44 David Hockney "A Bigger Splash" 1967;
Idols p43 (Robbie Williams); Index Stock Imagery Inc. pp12 (J.Koontz/Maria
Hernandez), 74 (P.Adams); PA Photos p20 (bank robbery); PhotoDisc pp20, 38,
45, 50, 54, 57, 77; Reuters News Media Inc. p43 (Julia Roberts); Scotland in
Focus p48 (B.Urquhart/Loch Ness); South American Pictures p13 (walking to
school); Stockbyte p25 (G.Doyle/man & woman)

CONTENTS

Auxiliary verbs • *have / have got*
Word formation • Words that go together
Prepositions – verb + preposition

It's a wonderful world!

Auxiliary verbs

1 The forms of *be*, *do*, and *have*

T 1.1 Read the sentences.

Present Simple
I speak Italian.
I don't speak Spanish.
Do you speak Italian?
My father speaks Italian.
My mother doesn't speak Italian.
Does your father speak Italian?

Continue these sentences in the same way.

Present Simple

1 I like skiing.

I _____ snowboarding.

_____ you _____ ?

My father _____ .

My mother _____ .

_____ your father _____ ?

Present Continuous

2 I'm studying English.

_____ Spanish.

_____

_____

_____

_____

Past Simple

3 I saw the Empire State Building.

_____ the Statue of Liberty.

_____

_____

_____

_____

Present Perfect

4 I've met Muhammad Ali.

_____ Pelé.

_____

_____

_____

_____

2 Full verb or auxiliary verb?

Read the sentences. Is the verb in bold an **auxiliary** verb (A) or a **full** verb (F)?

1 [A] **Have** you ever been to China?
2 [F] We **had** a lovely meal at Angie's.
3 [ ] **Did** anyone phone last night?
4 [ ] We **did** the washing-up before we went to bed.
5 [ ] She **has** coffee for breakfast every morning.
6 [ ] We **weren't** using your CD player, honestly!
7 [ ] Where **were** Andy and Lou at lunchtime?
8 [ ] Philippa never **does** her homework.
9 [ ] What **have** you done with my pen?
10 [ ] Why **are** you looking so sad?
11 [ ] We**'ve** got a new computer at home.
12 [ ] We **have** a new computer at home.

3 Contracted forms

Rewrite the sentences with contractions where possible.

1 I do not know where the post office is.
   I don't know where the post office is.

2 She has got two brothers and she does not get on with either of them.

_____

3 He has no brothers and sisters – he is an only child.

_____

4 We were not happy with the hotel so we did not stay there for long.

_____

5 He did not go to the party because he had a cold.

_____

6 They are getting married when they have saved enough money.

_____

7 John is not sure where Jill is.

_____

8 She is parking the car. It is always difficult in our street.

_____

9 I do not want them to know who I am.

_____

10 Do you not understand what I am saying?

_____

4 *My computer's gone wrong!*

1 **T 1.2** Complete the telephone conversation with auxiliary verbs. Use contractions where possible.

D Good afternoon, Computer Helpline, Damian speaking. How can I help you?

P Oh, at last! Hello, Damian. I (1) _____ got a real problem with my computer. It (2) _____ (not) working at all!

D OK, OK. Tell me your name and your company name and describe what (3) _____ happened.

P My name's Phil Evans. I (4) _____ (not) work for a company, I'm self-employed. I work at home, and I (5) _____ trying to meet an important deadline at the moment. This morning I (6) _____ working away happily, when suddenly everything stopped and a message came up on the screen. Then the screen went blank.

D OK Phil, (7) _____ (not) worry! What (8) _____ the message say?

P I can't remember exactly, because I (9) _____ (not) understand it, but I think it said something about 'not enough memory'.

D It's OK, Phil. I think I know what the problem is. Tell me, Phil, (10) _____ you switched the computer off?

P No, I (11) _____ (not). It's still on.

D Fine, Phil. Now do exactly what I say. Go to your computer, OK? Can you see a 'W' in the top right-hand corner? Click on that 'W' with the mouse. What (12) _____ it say? Can you read it to me?

P There's a list of three things. First it says …

2 Put the words in the correct order to make questions about the conversation. Then answer the questions.

1 Phil / the / is / why / Computer Helpline / ringing

_____?

Because _____

2 work / for / Phil / does / company / which

_____?

He _____

3 doing / when / computer / he / his / was / what / stopped

_____?

He _____

4 Phil / why / remember / message / the / can't

_____?

Because _____

5 switched / computer / he / has / his / off

_____?

No, _____

5 Making questions

Put the words in the correct order to make questions. Then answer them about you.

1 parents / where / were / your / born
   Where were your parents born?
   They were born in _____

2 moment / what / you / at / are / the / wearing

_____?

_____

3 play / any / the / at / sports / weekend / you / do

_____?

_____

4 up / time / morning / what / did / get / this / you

_____?

5 person / famous / ever / a / have / met / you

_____?

6 mother / look / your / you / like / do

_____?

7 go / you / where / holiday / were / did / child / when / you / on / a

_____?

6 Replying with questions

T 1.3 Reply to these statements with a suitable question.

1 Joan's writing an email.
   Who's she writing to?

2 David speaks four languages.

_____?

3 I got some lovely presents for my birthday.

_____?

4 Joy and Eric paid a lot of money for their house.

_____?

5 Bob's cat has just had kittens.

_____?

6 Jackie's going to the cinema on Saturday.

_____?

7 Marco's going shopping.

_____?

8 We had a wonderful holiday.

_____?

9 My job's really interesting.

_____?

10 Danka's talking on the phone.

_____?

7 Negatives and short answers

1 Complete the sentences with the correct auxiliary in the positive or negative.

1 Lizzie likes sushi, but Mark __doesn't__.

2 I don't like chocolate, but Petra __does__.

3 I've been to Korea, but Carlos _____.

4 Sandra isn't going to college, but I _____.

5 Leroy loves skateboarding, but we _____.

6 I heard the news last night, but my mother _____.

7 Ayako hasn't finished her work, but we _____.

8 I don't want to go to the gym, but they _____.

9 They didn't write to me, but you _____.

10 Your English is really improving, but mine _____.

2 Answer the questions about you with a short answer and some more information.

1 Do you speak three languages?

__Yes, I do. I speak French, German and Russian. /__

__No, I don't. I only speak two, French and Russian.__

2 Are you having a holiday soon?

_____

3 Did you have a good holiday last year?

_____

4 Have you ever been to Florida?

_____

5 Do you often travel abroad?

_____

6 Does your best friend sometimes go on holiday with you?

_____

Grammar revision

8 *have / have got*

! 1 *Have* and *have got* are both used for possession. *Have got* refers to the present and to all time, even though it looks like the Present Perfect.

> I**'ve got** two sisters.
> I **have** two sisters.
>
> She **has** blond hair.
> She**'s got** blond hair.

2 There are two forms for the question, the negative, and the short answer.

> **Have** you **got** any money? Yes, I **have**.
> **Do** you **have** any money? Yes, I **do**.
>
> He **hasn't got** a dog.
> He **doesn't have** a dog.

3 In all other tenses and verb forms, we use *have*, not *have got*.

> I **had** a bike when I was ten.
> I **didn't have** a car until I was twenty-five.
>
> I**'ve had** a headache all morning.
> I**'ll have** a steak, please.
>
> I love **having** a dog.
> I'd like **to have** another dog.

4 *Have*, not *have got*, is used for many actions and experiences.

> have breakfast / a cup of tea / a cigarette / a break / dinner
>
> have a bath / a shower / a rest
>
> have a swim / a good time / a party / a holiday
>
> have a chat / a row / a bad dream
>
> have a look at something / a word with someone
>
> have a baby

5 *Have got* is more informal. We use it more in spoken English. We use *have* more in written English. *Have* with *do/does* is more common in American English.

T 1.4 Complete the sentences with the correct form of *have* or *have got*.

1 Excuse me! <u>**Do you have**</u> / <u>**Have you got**</u> the time, please?

2 I'm starving. I <u>**didn't have**</u> anything to eat last night.

3 Peter, could you help me? I _____ a problem, and I don't know what to do.

4 **A** Why's Ann taking some aspirin?
   B Because she _____ a headache.

5 **A** Would you like tea or coffee?
   B I _____ a cup of tea, please.

6 **A** Can you lend me two euros?
   B Sorry. I _____ any money on me at all.

7 Maria _____ her baby. It's a girl. They're calling her Lily.

8 We _____ a party next Saturday. Would you like to come?

9 David! Can I _____ a word with you for a moment?

10 How was the party last night? _____ you _____ a good time?

11 **A** Excuse me! _____ a light, please?
    B Sorry. I don't smoke.

12 **A** What time _____ she usually _____ lunch?
    B About 1.00.

Vocabulary

9 Word formation

1 Look at these noun and adjective suffixes.

nouns	-ance	-ation	-ion	-ition	-ment	-ness

adjectives	-al	-ful	-tific	-ly	-ous	-y

Complete the charts.

Adjective	Noun
friendly	<u>friend</u>
_____	music
_____	science
happy	_____
_____	greed
_____	danger
wonderful	_____

Noun	Verb
invitation	<u>invite</u>
achievement	_____
_____	compete
discussion	_____
_____	organize
_____	appear
exploration	_____

2 Complete the sentences with words from exercise 1.

1 My family is very _____. My brothers play in a band and my mother is a concert pianist.

2 I'm having a birthday party this weekend and I'd like to _____ you.

3 My favourite _____ of the natural world is the Niagara Falls, without a doubt.

4 One of the most important _____ achievements is the discovery of penicillin.

5 Rock climbing is a _____ sport.

6 When we had a _____ about the film, we realized that nobody had enjoyed it.

7 Our dog wants to eat all the time – I don't know why he's so _____!

8 The Red Cross is a medical _____.

9 Yasmina entered a _____ in a magazine and won a holiday for two.

10 I've never been to Madrid before. Let's go out and _____.

10 Words that go together

Match a word in **A** with a line in **B**.

A	B
1 pay _e_	a lives
2 pop ___	b a coat
3 drive ___	c star
4 mobile ___	d abroad
5 save ___	e the bill
6 text ___	f an email
7 try on ___	g dangerously
8 send ___	h job
9 travel ___	i phone
10 part-time ___	j my friends

11 Grammar words

Match the words in **A** with a grammar term in **B**.

A	B
1 write, want _f_	a preposition (*prep*)
2 she, him ___	b adjective (*adj*)
3 car, tree ___	c adverb (*adv*)
4 can, must ___	d modal auxiliary verb
5 slowly, always ___	e pronoun (*pron*)
6 nice, pretty ___	f full verb
7 bigger, older ___	g countable noun (C)
8 to like ___	h uncountable noun (U)
9 a ___	i comparative adjective (*comp adj*)
10 on, at, under ___	j superlative adjective (*superl adj*)
11 hoping, living ___	k infinitive with *to* (*infin* with *to*)
12 the ___	l *-ing* form of the verb (*-ing* form)
13 fastest, hottest ___	m past participle (*pp*)
14 done, broken ___	n definite article (*def art*)
15 rice, weather ___	o indefinite article (*indef art*)

Pronunciation

12 Word stress

T 1.5 Put these words from Unit 1 of the Student's Book in the correct stress box.

wonderful	language	Japan
Olympics	information	breakfast
afford	believe	penicillin
business	computer	president
politician	happiness	important

A ●••

wonderful

_____

B ●•

language

_____

_____

C •●

Japan

_____

_____

D •●•

Olympics

_____

_____

E •••●•

information

_____

_____

13 Phonetic script

T 1.6 Read the poem and transcribe the words in phonetic script. There is a list of phonetic symbols on the inside cover of this book.

I Wonder

1 I wonder why /ðə grɑːs ɪz griːn/,

 And why the wind is never seen.

2 Who taught /ðə bɜːdz tə bɪld ə nest/,

 And told the trees to take a rest?

3 And when /ðə muːn ɪz nɒt kwaɪt raʊnd/,

 Where can the missing bit be found?

4 Who /laɪts ðə stɑːz/ when they blow out,

 And makes the lightning flash about?

5 Who paints /ðə reɪnbəʊ ɪn ðə skaɪ/,

 And hangs the fluffy clouds so high?

 Why is it now, do you suppose,

 That Dad won't tell me if he knows?

Jeannie Kirby

1 the grass is green

2 _____

3 _____

4 _____

5 _____

Prepositions

14 Verb + preposition

Complete the sentences with a preposition from the box.

of	about	to	in
with	for	on	

1 I think you're wrong. I don't agree
 _____ you at all.

2 I'm not interested _____ what you
 think of modern art.

3 You aren't concentrating on your work.
 What are you thinking _____ ?

4 What are you listening _____ ?

5 If you have a problem, talk _____
 the teacher.

6 **A** What did you talk _____ ?
 B Oh, this and that.

7 We might have a picnic tomorrow. It
 depends _____ the weather.

8 **A** What do you think _____ Pete?
 B I really like him.

9 Where's the cash desk? I'd like to pay
 _____ this book.

10 **A** I've lost your pen. Sorry.
 B It's all right. Don't worry _____ it.

11 **A** What are you looking _____ ?
 B My coat! Have you seen it?

12 **A** Bye. I'm off to that new restaurant.
 B Lucky you. Who are you going
 _____ ?

2

Present Simple • Present Continuous • Passive
Opposite adjectives • Phrasal verbs – *look* and *be*

Present Simple

1 Lives around the world

Look at the photographs. Then match the paragraphs with the people and put them in order.

Uma Singh and her husband Sanjit run a small corner shop in a suburb of New York.

☐ ☐ ☐

Thirteen-year-old **Maria Hernandez** lives with her family in Tuluca, Mexico.

☐ ☐ ☐

Vichai is 18. He lives in a town house with his family in Bangkok, Thailand.

☐ ☐ ☐

1 **His older sister** also lives at home. Their house is near the university, where he is in the second year of an engineering course. Lessons start at eight in the morning and go on until three in the afternoon, Monday till Friday. When he graduates, he wants to be a civil engineer.

2 '**My father** works in a car factory and my mother is a housewife. I'm the youngest of three children. We live in a small block of flats with five other families in the old part of town.'

3 'I usually have boiled rice for breakfast. Then at lunchtime I have chicken with fried rice or a bowl of noodles. I have lunch in the university cafeteria. In the evening I always eat with my family. My mother cooks. Her food's the best in the whole world!'

4 'Shops like these are like community meeting places. People come here to drink coffee, buy a newspaper or pass on messages. We even cash cheques for those people who don't have time to go to the bank.'

5 It takes her about 20 minutes to walk to school, but she usually goes by bus. Her school has a lot of students, with 30 or 40 girls and boys in each class.

6 At the weekend he earns some extra money teaching computer studies at a private computer school. He enjoys playing *takraw*, a Thai game played with a light ball made of rattan, which you can hit with your foot, knee, elbow or heel, but not your hand. He loves living in Bangkok, but he hates the traffic jams, which get worse every year.

7 'I go to school from Monday to Friday. Classes start at 8 a.m. and go on until 2 p.m. Our teachers speak Spanish and English. My school doesn't provide lunch so everybody brings a packed lunch. Sometimes I don't like school, but I have to study hard because I want to be an architect one day.'

8 **It sells** all sorts of food and household goods from sandwiches to washing-up liquid, from magazines to coffee and nails. 'We offer a huge range of products. It's like three or four shops rolled into one.'

9 The hours are very long. The shop opens at 6 a.m. and doesn't close until 11 p.m., except on Sunday when it's open from 8.30 a.m. until 5 p.m. Their whole lives are controlled by the shop. 'There are a lot of things we can't do any more. We don't go to the movies and we don't visit our friends at the weekend. But it's the long hours that make the money.'

2 Sentence completion

Complete the sentences about the people in exercise 1.

Uma and Sanjit

1 Uma and Sanjit _run_ a shop.
2 They _____ all sorts of food and household goods.
3 Most days the shop _____ until 11 p.m.
4 They _____ their friends any more.

Maria

5 Maria _____ one brother and one sister.
6 It _____ her 20 minutes to walk to school.
7 She _____ school at 2 p.m.
8 Her school _____ lunch.

Vichai

9 'When I _____, I _____ to be a civil engineer.'
10 'I _____ lunch in the university cafeteria.'
11 'I _____ extra money teaching computer studies.'
12 'I _____ the traffic in Bangkok.'

3 Questions

1 **T 2.1** Look at the answers to some questions about the people in exercise 1. Write the questions.

1 _____ ?
All sorts of food and household goods.

2 _____ ?
Six o'clock in the morning.

3 Why _____ movies any more?
Because they work such long hours.

4 _____ ?
In a car factory.

5 _____ ?
In a small block of flats.

6 _____ ?
Thirty to forty.

7 _____ ?
Spanish and English.

8 _____ ?
By bus.

9 _____ ?
She wants to be an architect.

10 Who _____ live _____ ?
With his parents and his sister.

11 _____ ?
Takraw.

12 _____ ?
Yes, he loves it, but he hates the traffic.

4 Negatives

Complete the sentences with a negative form of a verb plus the words in brackets.

1 Vegetarians **don't eat meat**. (meat)
2 An atheist _____. (God)
3 In Britain, police officers _____. (guns)
4 Selfish people _____. (other people)
5 Real Madrid football players _____. (red)
6 I'm unemployed. I _____. (job)
7 My father's bald. He _____. (hair)
8 They're penniless. _____. (money)
9 Kangaroos _____. (Mexico)

Pronunciation revision

5 -s at the end of a word

> ❗ **T 2.2** Remember the rules for the pronunciation of -s at the end of a word. This applies to the third person singular in the Present Simple and to plural nouns.
>
> 1 If the word ends in /s/, /z/, /ʃ/, /tʃ/, or /dʒ/, the final -s is pronounced /ɪz/.
>
> | | | | |
> |---|---|---|---|
> | misses | buses | chooses | sizes |
> | washes | dishes | watches | matches |
> | manages | badges | | |
>
> 2 If the word ends in /p/, /t/, /k/, /f/, or /θ/, the final -s is pronounced /s/.
>
> | | | | |
> |---|---|---|---|
> | stops | ships | hits | pets |
> | attacks | bricks | laughs | coughs |
> | maths | | | |
>
> 3 If the word ends in /b/, /d/, /g/, /v/, /ð/, /l/, /m/, /n/, /ŋ/, or any vowel sound, the final -s is pronounced /z/.
>
> | | | | |
> |---|---|---|---|
> | stabs | hands | bags | leaves |
> | breathes | hills | trams | earns |
> | goes | news | wears | songs |

T 2.3 The words in the box all appeared in the text about the people in exercise 1. Put them in the correct column.

cheques	girls	places	boys
lives	hours	earns	products
loves	minutes	closes	graduates
lessons	wants	messages	hates
cooks	sandwiches	things	

/s/	/z/	/ɪz/
cheques	_girls_	_places_

Present states and actions

6 Present Simple and Present Continuous

Read about Liam. Then write about Rita, Sally and Graeme in the same way.

At work

Liam is an actor. He sometimes makes films and sometimes works in the theatre. He often acts in Shakespeare plays and wears beautiful costumes. He doesn't earn a lot of money because he isn't very well-known.

Now

At the moment, he isn't working. He's relaxing at home. He's wearing jeans and a T-shirt and drinking coffee. He's waiting for the phone to ring because he needs more work.

At work

_____

_____

_____

_____

Now

_____

_____

_____

_____

At work

_____

_____

_____

_____

Now

_____

_____

_____

_____

Liam, actor — At work / Now

Rita, basketball coach — At work / Now

Graeme and Sally, organic farmers — At work / Now

7 Present Simple or Present Continuous?

1 Is the verb form in the sentences correct (✔) or incorrect (✘)?
Correct the wrong sentences.

1 ☐ I'm thinking you should go to the dentist.

2 ☐ What are you thinking of doing on Saturday?

3 ☐ Why do you leave so early? Don't you enjoy the party?

4 ☐ Nobody is ever laughing at my husband's jokes. It's so embarrassing.

5 ☐ I don't believe a word he says. He always tells lies.

6 ☐ We're seeing our bank manager at half past two.

7 ☐ I'm not seeing how I can help you.

8 ☐ Does this train stop at Oxford?

9 ☐ He's never knowing the answer.

2 **T 2.4** Put the verbs in the correct form, Present Simple or Present Continuous.

Conversation 1

A What (1) _____ (that man/do) over there?

B He (2) _____ (wait) for the bank to open.

A But the banks (3) _____ (not open) on Saturday afternoons.

B (4) _____ (you/think) he's a bank robber? Watch out! He (5) _____ (take) something out of his pocket. He (6) _____ (walk) towards us!

C Excuse me. Could you tell me the time, please?

Conversation 2

A What (7) _____ (you/do)?

B I (8) _____ (pack) my suitcase. I (9) _____ (leave) you and this house.

A But I (10) _____ (not/understand). Where (11) _____ (you/go)?

B I (12) _____ (not/know). The only thing I (13) _____ (know) is that Peter (14) _____ (meet) me at the airport at six o'clock.

3 Complete the pairs of sentences with the verb in brackets. Use the Present Simple for one and the Present Continuous for the other.

1 I _____ (think) of having a party.

 I _____ (think) that's a great idea!

2 _____ you _____ (see) what I mean?

 What time _____ you _____ (see) the doctor?

3 They _____ (have) a fantastic house.

 They _____ (have) a fantastic holiday.

8 Adverbs of frequency

Are the adverbs of frequency in the correct (✔) or incorrect (✘) places? Correct the wrong sentences.

1 ☒ Do usually you sit here?

   Do you usually sit here?

2 ☐ I have always liked Peter.

3 ☐ Never I have anything to eat in the morning.

4 ☐ I usually take my daughter to school.

5 ☐ I go sometimes abroad on business.

6 ☐ I have never enough money.

7 ☐ We often have tests in class.

8 ☐ Our teacher gives us always too much homework.

9 ☐ Sonja always is late for class.

Present passive

9 Past participles

Rewrite the sentences in the passive.

1 They speak English here.

   English is spoken here.

2 They produce Nokia phones in Finland.

   _____

3 They include service in the bill.

   _____

4 We are redecorating our kitchen at the moment.

   _____

5 They make champagne in France.

   _____

6 Another company is taking over our company.

   _____

7 The company employs about 1,000 people.

   _____

8 We grow all our vegetables on the farm.

   _____

9 They are pulling down that block of flats because it is unsafe.

   _____

   _____

10 They deliver our newspapers before breakfast.

   _____

10 Active or passive?

T 2.5 Complete the text with the correct form of the verbs, Present Simple active or passive.

Catching a plane

WHEN you (1) _____ (arrive) at an airport, you should go straight to the check-in desk where your ticket and luggage (2) _____ (check). You (3) _____ (keep) your hand luggage with you but your suitcases (4) _____ (take) to the plane on a conveyor belt. You can now go to the departure lounge. If you are on an international flight, your passport (5) _____ (check), and then your bags (6) _____ (x-ray) by security cameras; sometimes you (7) _____ (give) a body search and your luggage (8) _____ (search) by a security officer. You (9) _____ (wait) in the departure lounge until your flight (10) _____ (call) and you (11) _____ (tell) which gate number to go to. Finally, you (12) _____ (board) your plane and you (13) _____ (show) to your seat by a flight attendant.

Vocabulary

11 Opposite adjectives

Complete the chart. Use a prefix (*un-*, *in-*, *im-*) in the first column and a word from the box in the second column.

sad	casual	cheap	arrogant
cruel	rude	wrong	strange/rare
boring	stupid	ugly	out-of-date

Adjective	Opposite (prefix + adjective)	Opposite (different word)
1 happy	*unhappy*	*sad*
2 polite		
3 expensive		
4 interesting		
5 correct		
6 attractive		
7 fashionable		
8 intelligent		
9 usual		
10 kind		
11 formal		
12 modest		

Phrasal verbs

12 *look* and *be*

1 Look at the dictionary extracts of some phrasal verbs with *look*.

sb = somebody   sth = something

look after (sb/sth) to be responsible for or take care of sb/sth: *I want to go back to work if I can find somebody to look after the children.*
look for (sb/sth) to to try to find (sb/sth): *We looked for you everywhere. Where were you?* **look forward to sth/doing sth** to wait with pleasure for sth to happen (because you expect to enjoy it): *We're really looking forward to our holiday.* **look out** to be careful or to pay attention to sth dangerous, etc: *Look out! There's a car coming!* **look sth up** to search for information in a book: *to look up the times for trains to London.*

2 Complete the sentences using a phrasal verb with *look* in the correct tense.

1 If I don't know the meaning of a word, I **look** it **up** in the dictionary.

2 I'm _____ my glasses. Have you seen them?

3 _____ ! That glass is going to fall!

4 I _____ to seeing you next week.

5 **A** Do you know Kim's phone number?

   B Sorry, I don't. You should _____ it _____ in the phone book.

6 Babysitters _____ the children when the parents go out.

3 The verb *to be* is often followed by a particle to form a phrasal verb.

*Bye! I'm **off** to Australia for three weeks.* (= I'm going …)

Complete the sentences with a particle from the box. Some are used more than once.

on	up	in	up to	off	away

1 **A** Hello. Can I speak to Mr James, please?

   B I'm sorry. He isn't _____ at the moment. Can I take a message?

2 **A** Hello. Can I speak to Ms Richards, please?

   B I'm sorry. She's _____ on holiday at the moment.

3 **A** I feel like going to the cinema tonight.

   B Good idea! What's _____ at the moment?

4 I think this milk's _____ . It smells horrid.

5 **A** Where shall we go for dinner?

   B It's _____ you. It's your birthday. You choose.

6 Come on, kids! Aren't you _____ yet? Breakfast's on the table.

7 I wonder why they aren't answering the door. There must be someone _____ . All the lights are _____ .

8 I must be _____ soon. I want to get to the shops before they close.

9 **A** Why isn't my computer working?

   B Because the screen's _____ . That's why.

10 **A** You're crying. What's _____ ?

   B I'm just a bit sad. That's all.

3

Past tenses • *while, during,* and *for* • Past Perfect
Passive • Adverbs • Prepositions – *in, at, on* for time

Past Simple and Past Continuous

1 A sad story

1 Match the picture numbers with the verbs in the box.

Past Simple	Past Continuous
☐ ran up	☐ was waiting
☐ killed	☑ was watering the plants
☐ arrived	☐ were leaving
☐ put up	☑ was playing
☐ called	☐ were having tea
☐ rang	
☐ rescued	
☐ ran him over	
☐ couldn't get down	
☐ invited them in for tea	
☐ tried to tempt him down	

2 **T 3.1** Complete the story with the phrases from the box.

YESTERDAY EVENING, Mrs Taylor (1) **was watering the plants**
in her garden, while her cat, Billy, (2) _____ near
her. Suddenly, Billy (3) _____ a tree. Mrs Taylor
(4) _____ to Billy, but he (5) _____,
so she (6) _____ the Fire Brigade. While she
(7) _____ for them to arrive, she
(8) _____ with some fish. The
Fire Brigade eventually (9) _____,
(10) _____ their ladder and (11) _____
Billy. Mrs Taylor was so pleased that she (12) _____.
While they (13) _____, they didn't see Billy
go outside again, and ten minutes later as they
(14) _____, they (15) _____ and
unfortunately they (16) _____ him.

2 Correcting facts

Correct these false statements about the story.

1 The story happened last month.

   The story didn't happen last month.

   It happened yesterday evening.

2 Mrs Taylor was cutting the grass.

   _____

   _____

3 Billy was sleeping in the garden.

   _____

   _____

4 Billy jumped over the wall.

   _____

   _____

5 Mrs Taylor rang the Police.

   _____

   _____

6 The Fire Brigade used a rope to get Billy down.

   _____

   _____

3 Past Simple or Past Continuous?

Choose the correct form of the verb.

1 They _fell_ / _were falling_ in love when they _worked_ / _were working_ in Rome.

2 She _read_ / _was reading_ quietly in her room when suddenly the lights _went_ / _were going_ out and she _heard_ / _was hearing_ a scream.

3 He _stood_ / _was standing_ up, _walked_ / _was walking_ across the room, and _closed_ / _was closing_ the window.

4 A young woman _walked_ / _was walking_ into the office. She _carried_ / _was carrying_ a baby.

5 _Didn't you meet_ / _Weren't you meeting_ your wife while you _lived_ / _were living_ in Italy?

6 I _saw_ / _was seeing_ you in the park yesterday. You _sat_ / _were sitting_ with your arm round Tom.

7 As soon as I _walked_ / _was walking_ into the room, she _handed_ / _was handing_ me the letter.

8 His father was really angry with him because he _listened_ / _was listening_ to music while he _did_ / _was doing_ his homework.

9 Why _didn't they visit_ / _weren't they visiting_ me when they _stayed_ / _were staying_ in London?

10 What _did you write_ / _were you writing_ when your computer _crashed_ / _was crashing_?

4 A holiday in Florida

T 3.2 Complete the text with the correct form of the verbs, Past Simple or Past Continuous.

A special holiday in Florida

Last February, I (1) _decided_ (decide) to go on holiday to Florida. The day I (2) _____ (leave) England it (3) _____ (rain), but when I (4) _____ (land) in Florida, the sun (5) _____ (shine) and a lovely, warm breeze (6) _____ (blow) from the sea. I (7) _____ (take) a taxi to my hotel. As I (8) _____ (check in), someone (9) _____ (tap) me on the shoulder. I (10) _____ (can not) believe my eyes! It was my old girlfriend. She (11) _____ (stay) at the same hotel. The next day, we (12) _____ (go) snorkelling and (13) _____ (see) hundreds of beautiful fish. It (14) _____ (get) dark when we (15) _____ (return) to our hotel after a wonderful day. We (16) _____ (spend) the rest of the week together. It was very romantic. We (17) _____ (feel) very sad when the holiday (18) _____ (end).

5 What was he doing? What did he do?

Read the newspaper stories and answer the questions.

Hero saves man's life

Jack Easton, 38, was driving home from work at around 6.30 in the evening when he saw a yellow VW van, driven by Ken Sharpe, crash into a tree. Without thinking of his own safety, he pulled the young man out of the van and took him straight to hospital. The doctors say Ken will make a complete recovery.

1 What was Jack Easton doing when he saw the accident?
He was driving home from work.

2 What did Jack Easton do when he saw the accident?
_____

LOTTERY WIN FOR UNEMPLOYED MAN

Unemployed painter, John Phillips, received a very pleasant surprise last night. He was watching TV when a man from the lottery read the winning numbers. They were the numbers on John's ticket.  He had won £1,000,000. He immediately gave his wife a big kiss and took his whole family out for an expensive meal.

3 What was John Phillips doing when he heard the good news?
_____

4 What did John Phillips do when he heard the good news?
_____

Shock for bank customers Customers in the Whitehall Savings Bank received a terrible shock yesterday. People were standing in queues chatting to each other when two masked robbers burst into the bank. Sixty-year-old Martin Webb suffered a heart attack and was taken to hospital. The robbers escaped with £500,000.

5 What was happening in the bank when the robbers burst in?
_____

6 What happened to Martin Webb when the robbers burst in?
_____

Grammar revision

6 *while*, *during*, and *for*

❗ 1 *While* is a conjunction, and is followed by a clause.

> **While** I was getting ready, I listened to the radio.
> I met my wife **while** I was at university.

2 *During* is a preposition, and is followed by a noun. It tells us *when* something happened. It means *at some point in a period of time*.

> We had to call a doctor **during** the night.
> Can I speak to you **during** the break?

We cannot use *during* with a period of time.

> *We talked ~~during five minutes~~.
> *We're on holiday ~~during six weeks~~.

3 *For* is a preposition, and is followed by a noun. It tells us *how long* something lasts.

> We talked **for** five minutes.
> We're going on holiday **for** six weeks.

Complete the sentences with *while*, *during*, or *for*.

1 My uncle died **during** the war.

2 The phone rang _____ I was having supper.

3 I lived in Paris _____ several years.

4 _____ I was in Paris I made a lot of friends.

5 I was in hospital _____ three weeks.

6 _____ my stay in hospital, the nurses looked after me very well.

7 A football match lasts _____ ninety minutes.

8 I hurt my leg _____ I was playing football yesterday.

9 I hurt my leg _____ the second half of the match.

10 Traffic is always bad _____ the rush hour.

11 Last week I was held up _____ three hours because of the traffic.

12 Peter came round _____ we were eating.

13 Peter came round _____ the meal.

Past Perfect

7 Regular and irregular verbs

Complete the chart with the missing verb forms.

Infinitive	Past Simple	Past participle
grow	grew	grown
_____	_____	fallen
find	_____	_____
_____	_____	sold
feel	_____	_____
_____	_____	driven
fly	_____	_____
_____	left	_____
travel	_____	_____
lie (not tell the truth)	_____	_____
_____	_____	won
_____	spent	_____

8 Choosing the correct tense

T 3.3 Choose the correct tense in the story.

A Busy Day

I T WAS ten o'clock in the evening. Peter (1) *sat* / *had sat* down on his sofa and thought about the day. What a busy day it (2) *was* / *had been*. This was his first night in his own flat. He (3) *lived* / *had lived* his entire life in the family home, and now for the first time, he (4) *was* / *had been* on his own.

He sat surrounded by boxes that they (5) *didn't manage* / *hadn't managed* to unpack during the day. It (6) *took* / *had taken* months to get all his things together. His mother (7) *was* / *had been* very generous, buying him things like towels and mugs.

He (8) *went* / *had gone* into the kitchen and (9) *made* / *had made* a sandwich. He suddenly (10) *felt* / *had felt* very tired and yawned. No wonder he (11) *was* / *had been* tired! He (12) *was* / *had been* up since six o'clock in the morning. He (13) *decided* / *had decided* to eat his sandwich and go to bed. But he didn't get there …

9 Sentence completion

T 3.4 Complete the sentences with the words in brackets. Use the Past Perfect.

1 I was broke because I **had spent all my money on clothes**.
   (spend / money / clothes)

2 Jane was furious because she _____ _____ . (oversleep and miss the bus)

3 Mary was very disappointed with her son. He _____ .
   (not study enough and fail exams)

4 Before his accident, Peter _____ _____ . (be / best player / team)

5 I was very nervous as I waited in the departure lounge. I _____ .
   (never / fly / before)

6 Jack wanted a new challenge in his work. He _____ _____ .
   (do / same job / ten years)

7 I didn't know his name, but the face was familiar. I was sure _____ .
   (see / somewhere before)

8 When I got home, I was starving. I _____ _____ .
   (not have / anything to eat all day)

10 *had* or *would*?

Read the sentences. Does *'d* mean *had* or *would*?

1 I'd like a cup of coffee. **would**

2 I knew I'd seen the film before. **had**

3 You must try snowboarding! You'd love it! _____

4 She said she'd give him everything. _____

5 She said she'd given him everything. _____

6 I was tired because I'd been up since six. _____

7 I told you we'd arrive on time! _____

8 I told you they'd bought a house! _____

9 I didn't realize he'd already been there. _____

10 I'd give him a ring, if I were you. _____

Past Simple active and passive

11 Biographies

T 3.5 Complete the texts with the verbs in the boxes.

Helen Keller
a successful writer, who was deaf and blind (American, 1880–1968)

didn't know	toured	were caused	had
were told	taught	was made	came
was offered	found		

Helen Keller's deafness and blindness (1) **were caused** by a severe illness when she was a baby. Her parents (2) _____ what to do, and they (3) _____ it difficult to control their growing daughter. One day they (4) _____ about a brilliant young teacher called Anne Sullivan. She (5) _____ to work with Helen and, very firmly and patiently, (6) _____ her that every object (7) _____ a name. Eventually, Helen (8) _____ a place at university. After this, she (9) _____ the world helping people like herself. In 1962, the story of her life (10) _____ into a film, *The Miracle Worker*.

Charles Blondin
the world's most famous tightrope walker (French, 1824–1897)

became	died	fell	wasn't killed
walked	was born	was put	was taught
watched	were carried		

Charles Blondin (1) **was born** into a circus family. He (2) _____ to walk on a tightrope when he was five. In 1859, he (3) _____ very famous when a high wire (4) _____ above the Niagara Falls between America and Canada and he (5) _____ across it. Thousands of people (6) _____ him do it. Afterwards, many of them (7) _____ across the water on his back. Blondin sometimes (8) _____ from the high wire but he (9) _____ ; he (10) _____ peacefully in bed in his sleep!

Amy Johnson
the first woman pilot to fly to Australia (English, 1903–1941)

disappeared	held	was introduced	joined
didn't succeed	returned	were married	tried
was taught	was written		

Amy Johnson (1) **joined** the London Aeroplane Club when she was still a schoolgirl. There, she (2) _____ how to service planes and she (3) _____ to a pilot called Jim Mollison, who (4) _____ the record for a flight to Australia. In 1930, Amy (5) _____ to beat his record. She (6) _____ , but she was still the first woman to fly to Australia. When she (7) _____ , she and Jim Mollison (8) _____ . Amy was very popular and a song (9) _____ about her: *Amy, wonderful Amy!* Her death is a mystery. During the war, in 1941, she and her aeroplane (10) _____ into the sea.

12 Past passive

Rewrite the sentences using the passive.

1 Somebody broke my glasses.
   My glasses were broken.

2 Nobody asked him to come.
   He wasn't asked to come.

3 Somebody left the lights on.
   The lights _____ .

4 Somebody told me about it yesterday.
   I _____ .

5 Nobody invited her to the party.
   She _____ .

6 Somebody took us to the hospital.
   We _____ .

7 Nobody gave them any information.
   They _____ .

8 Did anybody find the missing child?
   Was _____ ?

9 Did anything disturb you in the night?
   Were _____ ?

13 was, were, did, or had?

Complete the sentences with was, were, did, or had.

1 The flight _____ delayed because of bad weather.

2 _____ you do much sightseeing when you visited Paris?

3 They _____ leaving for the train station when I last saw them.

4 I _____ forgotten to set my alarm clock, so I was late for work.

5 _____ it raining when you left the cinema?

6 The workers _____ told last night that the factory was closing.

7 The police found the money which _____ been stolen from the bank.

8 The fire _____ caused by an electrical problem.

9 She was surprised he knew her name. She _____ never met him before.

10 How many times _____ your passports checked before you got on the plane?

Vocabulary

14 Adverbs

Put the adverbs in the correct place in the sentences. Sometimes more than one place is possible.

1 The film was good.	*quite*
2 I phoned the police.	*immediately*
3 I got up late this morning, but I managed to catch the bus.	*just* *fortunately*
4 'Hi, Pete. How are you?' 'My name's John, but don't worry.'	*actually*
5 In the middle of the picnic it began to rain.	*suddenly*
6 I saw Mary at the party. I didn't see anyone else.	*only*
7 I gave a present to John, not to anyone else.	*only*
8 Jane and I have been friends. We went to school. We were born in the same hospital.	*even* *together* *always*
9 'I didn't like it.' 'I didn't like it.'	*either*
10 'I like it.' 'I like it.'	*too*

These sentences don't make sense without an adverb.

11 Everybody in our family loves ice-cream, me.	*really* *especially*
12 The traffic to the airport was bad that we missed the plane.	*nearly* *so*
13 I'm tall to be a policeman, but I haven't got qualifications.	*enough* *enough*

Pronunciation

15 Words that sound the same

T 3.6 In each sentence there are two words in phonetic script. They have the same pronunciation but different meanings and spellings. Write the words.

1 The King was /θrəʊn/ **thrown** off the /θrəʊn/ **throne** .

2 She /θruː/ _____ the ring /θruː/ _____ the window.

3 The soldiers /wɔː/ _____ khaki uniforms when they went to /wɔː/ _____ .

4 I must /wɔːn/ _____ you that ties must be /wɔːn/ _____ at the Ritz.

5 The police /kɔːt/ _____ the burglar and he ended up in /kɔːt/ _____ in front of Judge Jordan.

6 I /bluː/ _____ up six red balloons and ten /bluː/ _____ ones for the party.

7 We /njuː/ _____ that Sue and Jim had bought a /njuː/ _____ car.

8 I /sɔː/ _____ Jack at the doctor's. He had a /sɔː/ _____ throat.

9 The book I /red/ _____ on the train had a /red/ _____ cover.

10 We /rəʊd/ _____ our horses along the narrow /rəʊd/ _____ .

Prepositions revision

16 *in, at, on* for time

❶
1 We use *at* for times and certain expressions.
at 8.00	**at** midnight
at lunchtime	**at** the weekend
at Christmas	**at** the same time
at the moment	**at** the age of nine

2 We use *on* for days and dates.
on Friday	**on** Friday morning
on 12 September	**on** Saturday evening

3 We use *in* for longer periods such as months, years, and seasons.
in April	**in** 2002
in summer	**in** the nineteenth century

We say *at night* but *in the evening/afternoon*. We also say *I'll see you in the morning*, but *I'll see you tomorrow morning*.

4 There is no preposition before *last*, *next*, or *this*.
What did you do **last** night?
I'll see you **next** week.
We're going to the beach **this** weekend.

Complete the sentences with *in*, *at*, *on*, or — .

1 A I'm meeting Alan **—** this evening.
  B What time?
  A **At** six.

2 A What did you do _____ the weekend?
  B _____ Friday evening we went to a party. We slept in late _____ Saturday morning, and then _____ the afternoon we went shopping. _____ 7.00, some friends came round for a drink. We didn't do anything _____ Sunday. What about you?

3 The weather in England is unreliable. _____ summer it can be hot, but it often rains _____ April and June. _____ last year the summer was awful. The best English weather is usually _____ spring and autumn.

4 I learnt to drive _____ 1999 _____ the age of 17. My brother learnt _____ the same time as me, but I passed my test first.

5 I'll phone you _____ next week. _____ Thursday, maybe. _____ the afternoon. _____ about 3.00. OK?

6 I don't see my parents much. _____ Christmas, usually, and _____ the holidays.

4

Modal verbs 1 – obligation and permission • Word formation
Phrasal verbs – separable or inseparable?

Doing the right thing

have to / don't have to

1 *What do they have to do?*

1 Look at the photos. Match the statements with the people.

Jack, the teenager

Laura, the businesswoman

Rod, the retired man

1 | c | 'I have to wear smart suits.'

2 | | 'I always have to be home before midnight.'

3 | | 'My dad usually has to work in the evenings.'

4 | | 'I don't have to get up at 6.30 a.m. any more.'

5 | | 'My husband has to take our children to school every morning.'

6 | | 'My wife has to go to hospital every week.'

7 | | 'I have to get good marks in my exams.'

8 | | 'My little sister doesn't have to help with the housework.'

9 | | 'I often have to travel overseas.'

2 **T 4.1** Write the questions using the statements from exercise 1.

1 Why <u>do you have to wear smart suits?</u>

Because I have to meet a lot of important people.

2 Why _____?

Because I work for an international company.

3 Why _____?

Because my parents say that I have to.

4 Why _____?

Because I don't have to catch the 7.32 a.m. train to work.'

5 Why _____?

Because he's a teacher and he has to mark homework.

6 Why _____?

Because she broke her arm and she has to have physiotherapy.

7 Why _____?

Because my mum says that she is still too young.

8 Why _____?

Because I start work very early and he doesn't have to be at work until 9.30 a.m.

9 Why _____?

Because I want to go to a good university.

2 Forms of *have to*

Complete the sentences with a suitable form of *have to*.

1 I **'m having to** work very hard at the moment because I have an exam next week.

2 You **won't have to** work hard after your exam. You can have a holiday.

3 My aunt's a police officer so she _____ wear a uniform at work, but my uncle's a taxi driver so he _____ wear one.

4 When I was a teenager, we _____ be home by nine o'clock. But we _____ take as many exams as teenagers nowadays.

5 My teeth hurt when I drink something cold. I think I _____ see the dentist soon.

6 Nobody enjoys _____ get up at five o'clock in the morning.

7 _____ your grandfather _____ start work when he was only fourteen?

8 You _____ speak Russian to travel around Moscow, but it helps!

9 If you lose your job, _____ we _____ sell the car?

10 _____ we _____ have fish for supper again?

can and *be allowed to*

3 *Who says?*

1 Who says these sentences? Where are the people?

   1 'You can't park there. I'll give you a parking ticket.'
      A traffic warden in the street

   2 'I'm sorry, sir, but you can't get on the plane without a passport.'
      _____

   3 'You aren't allowed to look at your notes during the exam.'
      _____

   4 'Shh. You can't talk in here. People are studying.'
      _____

   5 'You can take your seat-belt off now and walk around, but you aren't allowed to smoke, and you can't use personal computers or mobile phones.'
      _____

   6 'We're allowed to make one phone call a week, and we can go to the library, but we spend most of the time in our cells.'
      _____

2 Write sentences about these places. Use *can* or *allowed to*.

   1 a restaurant
      You aren't allowed to play tennis in a restaurant.
      You can have a meal or drink coffee.

   2 a hospital
      _____
      _____

   3 a museum
      _____
      _____

   4 a swimming pool
      _____
      _____

   5 a cinema
      _____
      _____

4 Conversations asking permission

T 4.2 Look at the pictures of Jill and her father, Jack, and Sam, a businessman, and his boss Anna. Match the lines of the conversations with the correct person and put them in order.

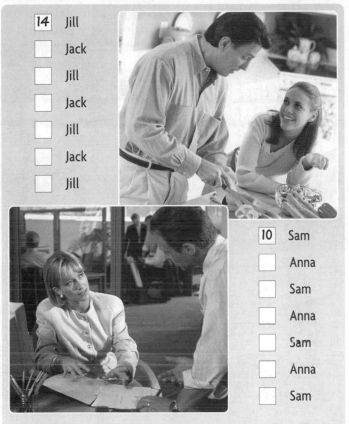

14	Jill
	Jack
	Jill
	Jack
	Jill
	Jack
	Jill

10	Sam
	Anna
	Sam
	Anna
	Sam
	Anna
	Sam

1 But I'm taking Dave to see his grandmother in hospital!
2 Yes, what is it?
3 I told you. *I* need it.
4 Well, it's not a very convenient time at the moment. We're very busy.
5 You know my father is having problems with his legs and he can't walk. Well, he needs to go into hospital next week, and I was wondering if I could have the day off.
6 Thanks a lot, dad. I won't be back late.
7 Oh, please! He won't be able to go if I don't give him a lift.
8 That's very kind. Thank you very much. I'm very grateful.
9 No, you can't. *I* need it.
10 Anna? Have you got a minute? Can I have a word?
11 I know we're busy, but he won't be able to get to the hospital if I don't take him.
12 All right. I suppose I can walk. The exercise will do me good.
13 Well, if that's the case then you must take him, of course.
14 Dad, can I have the car tonight?

should

5 Giving advice

1 Read the sentences and give advice. Use *should*.

  1 My son never wants to go out, he just plays computer games all day!
    You should tell him to get a job.

  2 My car keeps breaking down.
    _____

  3 I'm not sleeping very well these days.
    _____

  4 Since my mother died, my father doesn't know what to do with himself.
    _____

  5 I just don't know what to do with my hair. It looks awful!
    _____

2 Complete the questions with *should* and a suitable verb.

  1 Peter wants to go out with me. He's nice, but I only like him as a friend. **Should I go out** with him?
  2 I've been offered a place at Oxford and Cambridge. Which university _____?
  3 Everything on the menu looks wonderful! What _____ ?
  4 I want to tell Mike that he has bad breath, but I'm afraid of hurting his feelings. _____ or not?
  5 I've got a terrible headache, and I can't read the instructions on this aspirin bottle. How many _____ ?
  6 My aunt has invited me to her picnic, but I don't want to go. What _____ to her?

must and *have to*

6 *must* or *have to*?

Match the pairs of sentences with their meanings.

1 I must have a drink of water. **b**
  I have to drink lots of water. **a**

  a The doctor told me so.
  b I'm really thirsty.

2 I must do my homework tonight. ☐
  I have to do my homework tonight. ☐

  a I'm telling myself it's important.
  b This is why I can't come out with you tonight.

3 We must go to Paris sometime. ☐
  We have to go to Paris next week. ☐

  a Another boring business trip. Yawn.
  b It would be really nice.

4 I must wear something nice to go clubbing. ☐
  Men have to wear a shirt and tie to go into a
  posh restaurant. ☐

  a I want to look good.
  b It's the house rule.

5 I must water the plants today. ☐
  You have to water the plants daily. ☐

  a I haven't done them for ages.
  b They need lots and lots of water.

7 *mustn't* or *don't have to*?

Choose the correct verb form.

1 We have a lot of work tomorrow. You *mustn't* / *don't have to* be late.
2 You *mustn't* / *don't have to* tell Mary what I told you. It's a secret.
3 The museum is free. You *mustn't* / *don't have to* pay to get in.
4 Children *mustn't* / *don't have to* tell lies. It's very naughty.
5 Terry's a millionaire. He *mustn't* / *doesn't have to* go to work.
6 I *mustn't* / *don't have to* do my washing. My mother does it for me.
7 We *mustn't* / *don't have to* rush. We've got plenty of time.
8 You *mustn't* / *don't have to* play with guns. They're dangerous.
9 This is my favourite pen. You can borrow it, but you *mustn't* / *don't have to* lose it.
10 A Shall I come with you?
   B You can if you want, but you *mustn't* / *don't have to*.

8 Talking about obligation

Complete the sentences with *must*, *have to*, *mustn't*, or *don't have to*.

Vocabulary

9 Word formation

T 4.4 Complete the chart and add the stress. All the words appear in Unit 4 of the Student's Book.

	Noun	Verb
1	be'haviour	be'have
2		advise
3		introduce
4	invitation	
5		meet
6	relaxation	
7		discuss
8	refusal	
9	feeling	
10	gift	
11		bow
12	prayer	
13		invent
14		choose

	Noun	Adjective
15		national
16	tradition	
17	profession	
18		ill
19	value	
20	truth	
21		different
22		free
23	culture	
24	responsibility	
25		necessary

Pronunciation

10 Correcting wrong information

1 **T 4.4** Read the telephone conversation between Ms Maddox and the bank manager, Mr Sanders. When Ms Maddox corrects Mr Sanders, circle the stressed words.

Mr S Good morning, Mrs Maddox.

Ms M It's (Ms) Maddox, actually.

Mr S Oh yes. Ms Mary Maddox of ...

Ms M Ms Maureen Maddox.

Mr S Yes, of course. Now, Ms Maddox. I believe you want to borrow five hundred pounds.

Ms M No, in fact, I want to borrow five thousand pounds. Haven't you got my loan application?

Mr S No, I'm afraid not. But I understand you want to open a music shop for your son.

Ms M No, I want to open a flower shop for my daughter. Don't you think you should read my loan application, Mr Sanders?

Mr S A flower shop for your daughter. Well, I'll send you a form today ...

Ms M But you sent me a form last week, and I'm ringing because I have some queries about it.

Mr S Oh, so you've filled in the form ...

Ms M No, I haven't filled in the form. I can't fill it in because I don't understand it. That's why I'm ringing.

Mr S Oh I see! You want to ask me some questions about the form.

Ms M Not any more. I don't want to ask you questions about anything!! Goodbye!

2 Practise reading the conversation aloud.

Phrasal verbs

11 Separable or inseparable?

 A dictionary shows you whether a phrasal verb can be separated by an object.

> **turn sth on** to move the switch, etc. on a piece of machinery, etc. to start it working: *Turn the lights on!*

The preposition *on* comes after sth. This means the verb and the preposition can be separated.
Turn the light **on**. **Turn on** the light.

If the object is a pronoun (*it, him, her, me, them, us, you*), it must come before the preposition.

Turn **it** on.
NOT ~~Turn on it~~.

> **look for sb/sth** to try to find sb/sth: *We looked for you everywhere. Where were you?*

The preposition *for* comes before sb/sth. This means that the verb and the preposition cannot be separated.

> I'll **look for** John later. I'll **look for** him.
> NOT I'll look ~~him for~~.

T 4.5 Complete the sentences with the word *it* in the correct place. Use your dictionary for help.

1 You must be very hot with your coat on. Why don't you take __it__ off ___ ?

2 Your shirt is filthy! Just look ___ at ___ !

3 I haven't read the newspaper yet. Don't throw ___ away ___ .

4 The music is too loud! Turn ___ down ___ !

5 It'll be a great party! I'm really looking forward ___ to ___ .

6 Is that story about Ali true, or did you make ___ up ___ ?

7 I saw a lovely jumper today. I tried ___ on ___ but it was too small.

8 Don't drop your litter in the street! Pick ___ up ___ !

9 You can borrow my camera, but you must look ___ after ___ .

10 You can't have my dictionary. Give ___ back ___ to me!

5

Future forms • *somebody, nobody, anybody, everybody*
make or *do*? • Prepositions – *in*, *at*, *on* for place

On the move

Future forms 1

1 *will* or *going to*?

T 5.1 Complete the conversations with *will* or *going to* and the verb in brackets. Careful! Sometimes both forms are possible.

1 **A** Why are you wearing your old clothes?
   B Because I **'m going to wash** (wash) the car.

2 **A** I've got a headache. Have you got any aspirin?
   B Yes, they're in the bathroom. I
   _____ (get) some for you.

3 **A** Don't forget to tell me if I can help you.
   B Thank you. I _____ (give) you a
   ring if I think of anything.

4 **A** Why are you making sandwiches?
   B Because we _____ (have) a picnic
   on the beach.
   A What a lovely idea! I _____ (get)
   the towels and the swimming costumes.

5 **A** I'm going now! Bye!
   B Bye! What time _____ you
   _____ (be) back tonight?
   A I don't know. I _____ (call) you later.

6 **A** Who do you think _____ (win) the
   World Cup?
   B Brazil _____ (win), of course!

7 **A** You've still got my CD. Have you forgotten?
   B I'm sorry. Yes, I'd forgotten. I _____
   (fetch) it now.

8 **A** Dad, can you lend me ten pounds, please?
   I _____ (give) it back tomorrow.
   B I don't know. What _____ you
   _____ (do)?
   A I _____ (see) the new Tom Hanks
   film.

9 **A** Your exams start in two weeks' time. When
   _____ you _____
   (start) revising? You haven't done any revision yet.
   B I know. I _____ (do) some tonight.
   A You're going out tonight.
   B I _____ (start) tomorrow night, then.

10 **A** Can you take me to Harrods, please?
    B Yes, jump in.
    A How long _____ it
    _____ (take)?
    A About ten minutes.

11 **A** Do you like the shirt I bought for Peter's birthday?
    B Mmm. I'm sure he _____ (like) it,
    too.
    A What _____ you
    _____ (do) for his birthday?
    B We're going out for a meal.

2 *Where are they going?*

Look at the pictures. Where are the people going? Write questions and answers with *going* + verb + *-ing*.

1 Where's he going?

He's going swimming.

2 _____

_____

3 _____

_____

4 _____

_____

5 _____

_____

6 _____

_____

3 *I'm sure they'll ...*

Complete the sentences. Use *will* or *won't*.

1 Tomoko's been studying very hard for her exams. I'm sure she'll pass the exams easily.

2 If you don't feel well, go to bed and rest. I'm sure you _____ soon.

3 Ask John if you have problems with your homework. I'm sure _____ you.

4 I'll ask my sister for some money, but I know she _____ . She's very mean.

5 You don't need your umbrella today. I don't think _____ .

6 Don't sit in the sun for too long. You _____ .

7 Don't go to that new restaurant. I'm sure you _____ .

4 Making offers

T 5.2 Make offers with *I'll* for these situations.

1 **A** It's so hot in this room!

B I'll open the window. _____

2 **A** I'm so thirsty!

B _____

3 **A** There's someone at the door.

B _____

4 **A** I don't have any money.

B _____

5 **A** I need to be at the station in ten minutes.

B _____

6 **A** My suitcases are so heavy!

B _____

Future forms 2

5 Making arrangements

T 5.3 Complete the conversation with the Present Continuous form of the verbs in the box.

invite	drive	have	make	stay
get	bring	give	travel	deliver

Ssh! Can you keep a secret?

A Can you keep a secret?

B Yes, of course. What is it?

A I (1) _'m having_ a surprise party for Rosa next Saturday. It's her thirtieth birthday.

B A surprise party! That'll be difficult to arrange without her knowing. Who (2) _____ you _____?

A Everybody. All our friends, her friends from work, all her family, even her two aunts from Scotland. They (3) _____ down on Friday evening and they (4) _____ her cousins with them.

B What about the food and drink? Where (5)_____ you _____ that from?

A It's all arranged. Marcello's restaurant (6) _____ all kinds of food and drink on Saturday afternoon, and their chef (7) _____ even _____ a special birthday cake with pink icing and sugar flowers.

B Excellent! And what (8) _____ you _____ Rosa for her birthday? Have you got her a good present?

A Oh yes! I've booked a very special holiday. A week for two in Bali! We (9) _____ first class and (10) _ _____ in a five-star hotel.

B That's a great idea. Very clever! I can see that you're going to enjoy her birthday, too! Am I invited to this party?

A Of course. But keep it a secret!

6 Choosing the correct form

Choose the correct form of the verb.

1 **A** Have you got toothache again?

 B Oooh! It's agony! But I *see* / *'m seeing* the dentist this afternoon.

2 **A** Have you booked your holiday?

 B Yes, we have. We *'re going* / *'ll go* to Italy.

3 **A** What a beautiful day! Not a cloud in the sky!

 B Ah, but the weather forecast says it *'s raining* / *'s going to rain.*

4 **A** Please don't tell anyone. It's a secret.

 B Don't worry. We *won't tell* / *'re not telling* anybody.

5 **A** I haven't got enough money to pay for my ticket.

 B It's OK. I *'m going to lend* / *'ll lend* you some.

6 **A** You two look really shocked. What's the matter?'

 B We've just learnt that we *'ll have* / *'re going to have* twins!

7 **A** I thought you had just bought a new dishwasher.

 B Yes, that's right. It *'s being* / *will be* delivered tomorrow.

8 **A** Can you meet me after work?

 B I'd love to, but John *'s taking* / *'ll take* me out for dinner tonight.

Grammar revision

7 *somebody, nobody, anybody, everybody*

❗ 1 Look at the sentences from the text about Karen Saunder's job on p43 of the Student's Book.

> My ideal holiday has a little bit of **everything**.
> … I need to do **something**.

2 Look at the compounds that can be formed.

some any no every	+	one body thing where }

3 In general, we use *some* in positive sentences and *any* in negatives and questions, but not always. In offers and requests, we usually use *some*.

> Would you like **something** to eat?
> Can I have **something** to drink?

We use *some* when we expect the answer 'yes'.

> Is there **somebody** I can speak to?
> Can we go **somewhere** quiet?

4 We generally use *any* after *if*.

> If you need **anything**, just ask.

5 *Any* has another meaning. It can mean: *It doesn't matter who/where/what …*

> Come and see me **anytime** you want. I don't mind.
> Help yourself to food. You can have **anything** you want.
> **Anyone** will tell you that two and two is four.

Complete the sentences with a compound word.

1 Does **anyone** want a game of tennis?

2 What's that smell? Can you smell **something** burning?

3 I asked if _____ wanted an ice-cream, but _____ did, so I just bought one for myself.

4 Did _____ phone me while I was out?

5 Your face looks terribly familiar. Haven't I seen you _____ before?

6 She left the room without saying _____ .

7 This doesn't look like a very nice restaurant. Can we go _____ else?

8 I have _____ more to say to you. Goodbye.

9 **A** Where do you want to go on holiday?

   B _____ with a beach. I don't care where it is as long as it's sunny and has got a nice beach!

10 I felt so embarrassed. I was sure that _____ was looking at me.

11 **A** What do you want for supper?

    B _____ . I don't mind.

12 It was Sunday, and the town was deserted. _____ was in the streets, and _____ was open.

13 **A** Who was at the party?

    B _____ . Pete, Anna, James, Kathy, all the Smiths, Sally Beams, and Sally Rogers.

14 I have never been _____ more beautiful than Scotland.

Vocabulary

8 *make* or *do*?

1 Which expressions go with *make*, and which go with *do*? Write them in the correct columns.

	make	do
a mistake	a mistake	my homework
my homework		
up your mind		
the shopping		
a decision		
a mess		
a complaint		
someone a favour		
sure that		
the housework		
my bed		
nothing		
my best		
money		
a speech		
a profit		
exercises		
a noise		
a phone call		
friends with		
the washing-up		
progress		

2 Complete the sentences using the expressions from exercise 1 in the correct form.

1 First she said yes, then she said no, but in the end she _____ to marry him.

2 I like to keep fit, so I _____ every day.

3 I love Sundays! I can lie on the sofa all day and _____ .

4 Ssh! You mustn't _____ . The baby's asleep.

5 My teacher says I must work harder, but I can't work any harder, I'm _____ .

6 We asked to see the manager and we _____ about the terrible service in the restaurant.

7 We have an agreement in our house. I cook dinner every evening and afterwards James _____ .

8 Could you _____ please? Could you give me a lift to the airport?

9 When I got married, my father stood up and _____ where he thanked everybody for coming and making the day so special.

10 We have some lovely new neighbours. We've already _____ them.

11 Is there a public call box near here? I have to _____ .

12 Before you go on holiday you should _____ all the doors and windows are locked.

Pronunciation

9 Vowel sounds and spelling

1 **T 5.4** Circle the symbol that matches the sound in the underlined letters. They are all single vowel sounds.

1	w<u>or</u>d	/ʌ/	(/ɜː/)	/ɔː/
2	w<u>ea</u>ther	/e/	/iː/	/æ/
3	s<u>u</u>gar	/uː/	/ʊ/	/ʌ/
4	w<u>o</u>man	/ɒ/	/ɪ/	/ʊ/
5	w<u>o</u>men	/ɒ/	/ɪ/	/ʊ/
6	<u>u</u>ncle	/ʌ/	/æ/	/ʊ/
7	h<u>al</u>f	/ɑː/	/æ/	/ɔː/

2 **T 5.5** Cross out the word which does not contain the vowel sound.

1	/ɪ/	build	~~field~~	fill	women
2	/e/	leather	friend	break	bread
3	/ʌ/	front	rough	won't	country
4	/ɒ/	clock	wonder	want	wash
5	/æ/	angry	hungry	fax	salmon
6	/iː/	cheese	breath	meal	breathe
7	/uː/	spoon	wooden	zoo	souvenir
8	/ɔː/	warm	walk	store	work
9	/ɜː/	world	ferry	early	journalist

3 **T 5.6** Transcribe these words from the article on p43 of the Student's Book.

1	/biːtʃ/	**beach**
2	/ɪkˈsplɔrɪŋ/	_____
3	/ˈtʃɜːtʃɪz/	_____
4	/mjuːˈziːəmz/	_____
5	/ˈrestrɒnts/	_____
6	/ˈfeɪvərɪt/	_____
7	/dɪˈlɪʃəs/	_____
8	/ˈdɪfrənt/	_____
9	/ˈskʌlptʃəz/	_____
10	/ˈdʒuːəlri/	_____

Prepositions revision

10 *in*, *at*, *on* for place

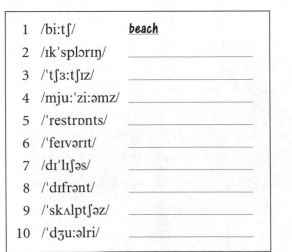

1 *In* is used to express a position inside a place. It suggests three dimensions.

> He works **in** an office in London.
> He lives **in** the south of England.
> He potters **in** the garden.
> There are lots of shops **in** the airport.

2 *At* is used to express a location at a point. It suggests two dimensions.

> Lucinda's **at** home. Justin's **at** Ben's house.
> I'll see you **at** the cinema at 8.00.
> I've left my case **at** the office.
> We arrived **at** the airport with time to spare.

3 *On* is used to talk about position on a surface.

> This exercise is **on** page 36.
> We drive **on** the left.
> There are no pictures **on** the wall.
> Our flat is **on** the third floor.

Complete the sentences with *in*, *at*, or *on*.

1 I met my husband ____ Italy. He was ____ a shop, buying pasta. I was ____ the queue, waiting to buy some bread.

2 Last night when I was ____ the kitchen, I couldn't find my glasses. I looked ____ all the shelves and ____ all the cupboards. I thought I'd put them ____ one of the drawers, but they weren't there. They certainly weren't ____ the table or ____ the floor. Had I left them ____ work? Were they ____ the car? Then I realized where they were. They were ____ top of my head!

3 **A** Where were you at two o'clock yesterday?
   B ____ the beach.
   C ____ work.
   D ____ Manchester.
   E ____ Sally's house doing my homework.
   F ____ the bath.
   G ____ home.
   H ____ a boat.

6

like • Verb patterns • Antonyms and synonyms
Phrasal verbs – phrasal verb + object

I just love it!

like

1 Questions with *like*

1 Answer the questions about yourself.

1 What do you like doing most in your English class?

_____

2 Do you like working alone or with a partner?

_____

3 Would you like to have more or less homework after class?

_____

4 What's your classroom like?

_____

5 What are your classmates like?

_____

6 What is your spoken English like?

_____

7 Would you like to speak more or write more in class?

_____

2 Write questions using the phrases in the box.

> Do … like …?
> What … like?
> Would … like …?
> What/Who … look like?
> How …?

1 **What's the weather like?**

It's raining again!

2 **Do you like cooking?**

No, I don't. I can't even boil an egg!

3 _____ ?

Well, it's pressured and the hours are so long. But it pays well, I suppose.

4 _____ in your family?

Well, everybody says I look like my mother but I think I look more like my father.

5 _____ as a child?

I looked quite funny. I was very tall and thin. My nickname was 'The Pencil'!

6 _____ ?

Coffee, please. I don't like tea.

7 _____ tennis ?

Yes, I love it. I play every weekend in summer.

8 _____ ?

Yes, I'd love to. What time does the film start?

9 _____ . ?

Well, it's quite old, but with a modern kitchen, and it has a lovely garden.

10 _____ ?

Mum's in New York at the moment. But they're both very well, thank you. I'll tell them you asked about them.

3 **T 6.1** Read the conversation between two friends. Complete it with questions.

A I'm applying for a job in East Africa.

B Are you? I used to live there. In Tanzania. I was there about ten years ago.

A Really! (1) What _____ ?

B It was really interesting. I was there for two years. I liked everything except the climate.

A Why? (2) _____ that _____ ?

B Well, I was on the coast, in Dar es Salaam, so it was very hot and humid all of the time.

A And the people, (3) _____ ?

B Very nice. Very kind. And of course the Masai people look wonderful.

A (4) _____ ?

B Well, they're very tall and they wear the most amazing coloured beads, in their hair, round their necks, on their arms and legs. And the unmarried men put red mud in their hair. They're a magnificent sight.

A I suppose you went on safari when you were there. (5) _____ that _____ ?

B I loved it. It was very exciting. I went to the Serengeti Plain and the Ngoro Ngoro Crater.

A (6) Which animals _____ best?

B Actually, I think it was the giraffes. They were so graceful, so elegant – but I liked all the animals. (7) What _____ to see if you go there?

A The lions, of course. Especially those that live in the trees. I hope I get the job. It's been great talking to you.

B And you. Give me a ring and let me know what happens.

2 *like* or *would like*?

1 Match a sentence in **A** with a sentence in **B**.

A	B
1 I like brown bread. _e_	a I'd love one. I'm very thirsty.
2 Would you like a lift? ___	b I hate it.
3 Would you like some more apple pie? ___	c I'd love to. That's very kind.
4 Would you like a cold drink? ___	d I'd love some. It's delicious.
5 Don't you like football? ___	e I don't. I can't stand it.
6 I don't like jazz. ___	f Neither would I.
7 I wouldn't like to live in a city. ___	g Nothing.
8 Would you like to come to the theatre with us? ___	h Really? I love it.
9 What do you like doing on Sundays? ___	i It's OK. I think I'll walk.

2 **T 6.2** Tick the correct question.

1 A ☑ Where do you like going on holiday?
      ☐ Where would you like to go on holiday?
   B We usually go skiing in the winter, then somewhere hot in the summer.

2 A ☐ What do you like to do tonight?
      ☐ What would you like to do tonight?
   B Something a bit different. I feel like a change.

3 A ☐ Where do you like going on holiday?
      ☐ Where would you like to go on holiday?
   B Somewhere hot! I want to get brown.

4 A ☐ Do you like ice-cream?
      ☐ Would you like an ice-cream?
   B No, thanks.

5 A ☐ What sort of music do you like listening to?
      ☐ What sort of music would you like to listen to?
   B Classical, usually.

6 A ☐ Do you like swimming?
      ☐ Would you like to go swimming?
   B It's OK, but I get bored.

7 A ☐ Do you like swimming?
      ☐ Would you like to go swimming?
   B Great! Let's go.

8 A ☐ Would you like to be a teacher?
      ☐ Do you like your teacher?
   B I couldn't stand it!

Grammar revision

3 *like* and *as*

> **❶**
> 1 When *like* is used as a preposition, it is always followed by a noun. It means *similar to / the same as*.
>
> > I look **like** my mother.
> > They have so many animals. Their house is **like** a zoo.
> > 'What star sign are you?' 'I'm Gemini, **like** you.'
> > 'You're stupid.' 'Why do you say things **like** that?'
>
> 2 We use *as* in comparisons.
>
> > My daughter is **as** tall as me.
> > She works in the same office **as** me.
>
> 3 When *as* is used as a conjunction, it is followed by a subject and a verb.
>
> > Do **as** I say and sit down.
> > Don't eat and speak at the same time, **as** my mother used to say.
> > **As** you know, we're leaving tomorrow at 10.00.
>
> 4 Notice the use of *as* in *as usual*.
>
> > Pat and Peter arrived late, **as** usual.

Complete the sentences with *as* or *like*.

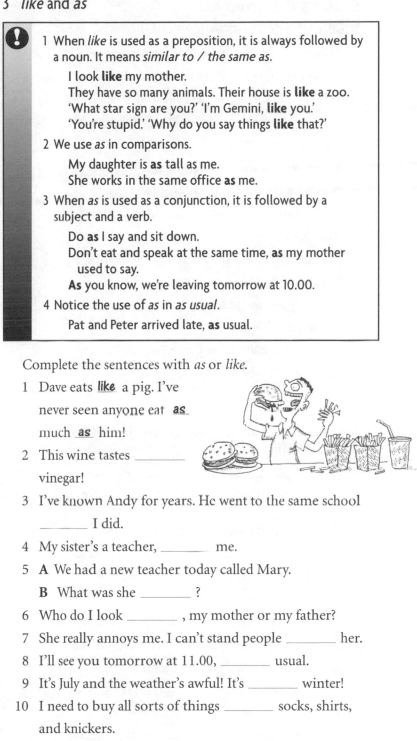

1 Dave eats **like** a pig. I've never seen anyone eat **as** much **as** him!

2 This wine tastes _____ vinegar!

3 I've known Andy for years. He went to the same school _____ I did.

4 My sister's a teacher, _____ me.

5 A We had a new teacher today called Mary.
   B What was she _____ ?

6 Who do I look _____ , my mother or my father?

7 She really annoys me. I can't stand people _____ her.

8 I'll see you tomorrow at 11.00, _____ usual.

9 It's July and the weather's awful! It's _____ winter!

10 I need to buy all sorts of things _____ socks, shirts, and knickers.

11 I'll be back in touch _____ soon _____ possible.

12 My brother has a car _____ yours.

13 Don't touch anything. Leave everything _____ it is.

14 It's freezing. My feet are _____ blocks of ice.

Verb patterns

4 Choosing the correct form

T 6.3 Choose the correct form of the verb.

1 I want *you be / you to be / that you are* more careful with your homework in the future.

2 I stopped *to smoke / smoke / smoking* when I was 25.

3 Why did I promise *help / to help / helping* with the painting? I hate it!

4 I tried *tell / to tell / telling* you that you were making a mistake, but you wouldn't listen.

5 I'm looking forward *go / to go / to going* to Sydney next year.

6 My father let me *having / to have / have* driving lessons when I was seventeen.

7 Mike invited me to his party, but I wasn't allowed *go / to go / going*.

8 I finished *watching / to watch / watch* TV and then I went to bed.

5 *-ing* forms

Complete the sentences with the *-ing* form of the verbs in the box.

walk	give up	hear	mend	work
help	wake up	find	watch	live

1 I'm tired of **hearing** nothing but bad news.

2 _____ too much TV is bad for your eyes.

3 I'll repair your watch for you. I'm good at _____ things.

4 _____ a good job these days is really difficult.

5 My children are afraid of _____ in the dark now, so we keep a light on at night.

6 Did you know that _____ is one of the best forms of exercise?

7 Thank you for _____ me. I really appreciate it.

8 _____ in a big city can be very stressful.

9 _____ smoking is easy. I've done it hundreds of times!

10 I earned a lot of money by _____ overtime.

6 Infinitive or *-ing* form?

Complete the sentences with the infinitive or *-ing* form of the verbs in the box. Write your answers in the puzzle. The vertical words spell what we all like to eat (9, 4)!

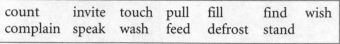

count	invite	touch	pull	fill	find	wish
complain	speak	wash	feed	defrost	stand	

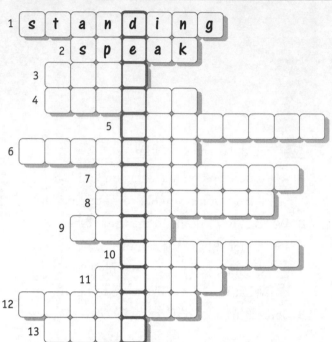

1 I hate **standing** in a queue. It's such a waste of time.

2 My baby daughter is just learning to **speak**. She can say two words – 'Mama' and 'pussy'.

3 Can you remember to _____ up the car with petrol? It's nearly empty.

4 I'd love to _____ Dave and Maggie round for a meal some time.

5 I couldn't sleep last night. I tried _____ sheep, but that didn't help.

6 My jeans need _____ . They're filthy.

7 The customer tried to _____ about the service in the restaurant, but the waiter refused to listen.

8 Stop _____ my hair! It hurts!

9 I just want to _____ you a happy birthday.

10 Would you mind _____ our cat while we're away on holiday?

11 When you go round a museum, you aren't allowed to _____ anything.

12 Don't forget to _____ the chicken before you cook it.

13 Did you manage to _____ what you were looking for?

7 Using a dictionary

Look at the extracts from the Oxford Wordpower Dictionary. They show you all the possible verb patterns. Is the verb pattern correct (✔) or incorrect (✗)? Rewrite the incorrect ones.

> ★ **like**[1] /laɪk/ **verb** [T] (not in the continuous tenses) **1** to find sb/sth pleasant; to be fond of sb/sth: *He's nice. I like him a lot.* • *Do you like their new flat?* • *I like my coffee with milk.* • *I like playing tennis.* • *She didn't like it when I shouted at her.* ··➤ opposite **dislike**.
> ➤ When **like** means 'have the habit of…' or 'think it's a good thing to…', it is followed by the infinitive: *I like to get up early so that I can go for a run before breakfast.*
> ··➤ Look at **likes** and **dislikes**. **2** to want: *Do what you like. I don't care.*
> ➤ **Would like** is a more polite way to say 'want': *Would you like to come to lunch on Sunday?* • *I would like some more cake, please.* • *I'd like to speak to the manager.* **Would like** is always followed by the infinitive, never by the *-ing* form.
> **3** (in negative sentences) to be unwilling to do sth: *I didn't like to disturb you while you were eating.*

like

1. ✔ We like walking by the river at weekends.
2. ☐ Would you like coming round to our house for dinner?
3. ☐ I like it that you laugh at my jokes.
4. ☐ I like to go to the gym three times a week.
5. ☐ I'd like to order a taxi.
6. ☐ I'm afraid I dislike my new boss.

> ★ **agree** /ə'griː/ **verb 1** [I,T] **agree (with sb/sth)**; **agree (that…)** to have the same opinion as sb/sth: *'I think we should talk to the manager about this.' 'Yes, I agree.'* • *I agree with Paul.* • *Do you agree that we should travel by train?* • *I'm afraid I don't agree.* ··➤ Look at **disagree**. **2** [T] **agree (to sth)** to say yes to sth: *I asked if I could go home early and she agreed.* • *Andrew has agreed to lend me his car for the weekend.* ··➤ Look at **refuse**. **3** [I,T] **agree (to do sth)**; **agree (on sth)** to make an arrangement or agreement with sb: *They agreed to meet again the following day.* • *Can we agree on a price? We agreed a price of £500.* **4** [I] **agree with sth** to think that sth is right: *I don't agree with experiments on animals.* **5** [I] to be the same as sth: *The two accounts of the accident do not agree.*

agree

7. ☐ Alan thinks it's too expensive, and I'm agree.
8. ☐ She thinks she's right, but I'm not agree.
9. ☐ I don't agree with you.
10. ☐ All doctors agree that smoking is bad for your health.
11. ☐ She thought we should go, and I agreed it.
12. ☐ They agreed talking about it again tomorrow.

Vocabulary

8 Antonyms and synonyms

1 Write the opposite.

1 an old man   <u>a young man</u>
   an old house   <u>a new house</u>

2 a single person _____
   a single ticket   _____

3 a light colour   _____
   a light suitcase _____

4 a hard test   _____
   a hard pillow   _____

5 a short film   _____
   a short man   _____

6 a hot curry   _____
   a hot drink   _____

7 dark hair   _____
   a dark room   _____

2 Write another adjective with a similar meaning.

1 a pretty girl   <u>an attractive girl</u>
2 a handsome man   <u>a good-looking man</u>
3 a rich woman   _____
4 a funny story   _____
5 an untidy room   _____
6 accurate information _____
7 friendly people   _____
8 a silly person   _____
9 a clever person   _____
10 a wonderful idea   _____
11 awful news   _____
12 disgusting food   _____

Pronunciation

9 Sentence stress

T 6.4 What did **A** say? Look at the stressed words in **B**'s reply and complete **A**'s statement or question.

1 **A** Jack <u>is very short</u>.

  B No, he isn't. Jack's very *tall*.

2 **A** Anna's got _____

  B No, she hasn't. Anna's got *short*, blonde hair.

3 **A** _____ ?

  B No, I don't. I want a *return* ticket.

4 **A** _____ ?

  B No, she doesn't. Liz likes *white* wine.

5 **A** _____ ?

  B No, he didn't say that. He said the film was *interesting*.

6 **A** _____ ?

  B No, they don't. Jane and Paul *hate* going for walks.

7 **A** _____ ?

  B No, thanks. I'd like a *cold* drink, please.

8 **A** _____ ?

  B No, I haven't. I've got a *stomach* ache.

9 **A** _____

  B Well, I *hated* school when I was a child.

Phrasal verbs

10 Phrasal verb + object

1 Match a verb in **A** with an object in **B**.

A		B	
1	sort out _d_	a	clothes in a shop
2	put out ___	b	children
3	fill in ___	c	the answer
4	find out ___	d	a problem
5	try on ___	e	the television
6	try out ___	f	toys in the cupboard
7	bring up ___	g	a form
8	clear up ___	h	something you don't want to a shop
9	take back ___	i	a new idea, a new drug
10	work out ___	j	a fire
11	put away ___	k	information
12	turn off ___	l	a mess

2 Complete the sentences with one of the phrasal verbs in its correct form.

1 I'll dry the dishes if you **put** them **away**. I don't know where they go.

2 **A** Can you _____ the time of the next train to London?

  B OK. I'll phone the station.

3 **A** What should I do with this form?

  B Just _____ it _____ and give it to the receptionist.

4 **A** Oh, dear! The washing machine isn't working, I haven't got any clean clothes, and I've got to go to work. What am I going to do?

  B Don't worry. I'll _____ it all _____ . Just go to work.

5 The fire was so intense that it took the firemen three hours to _____ it _____ .

6 The government wants to _____ a new scheme to encourage people to start their own businesses.

7 **A** Can I _____ these jeans _____ , please?

  B Sure. The changing rooms are over there.

8 That maths exam was really hard. It took me ages to _____ some of the answers.

9 I don't mind you baking a cake, but just make sure you _____ everything _____ when you've finished.

10 **A** Look at these shoes! They're brand new, and the heel's fallen off already.

  B _____ them _____ and change them, then.

7

Present Perfect active and passive
Tense review • Words with more than one meaning
Prepositions – noun + preposition

The world of work

Present Perfect

1 *How many did she ...? How many has she ...?*

1 Complete the questions with the Present Perfect or the Past Simple.

Margaret Atwood • 1939–

a How many books
has she written?

Jane Austen • 1775–1817

b How many books
did she write?

Julia Roberts • 1967–

c How many films
?

Marilyn Monroe • 1926–1962

d How many films
?

Bob Marley • 1945–1981

e How many records
_____?

Robbie Williams • 1974–

f How many records
_____?

David Hockney • 1937–

g How many pictures
_____?

Vincent Van Gogh • 1853–1890

h How many pictures
_____?

2 Match the sentences and the people.

1 [c] She has been one of the world's most popular actresses for many years.

2 [ ] He has lived in Los Angeles for many years because he prefers the light there.

3 [ ] She has won many awards for her writing.

4 [ ] He has had a successful solo career since leaving the boy band, *Take That*.

5 [ ] She committed suicide in 1962.

6 [ ] His band was called *The Wailers*.

7 [ ] She never married.

8 [ ] He only sold one painting while he was alive.

3 Ask questions about the first four sentences in exercise 2.

1 When **did she make** her first film?

2 Why _____ to Los Angeles?

3 When _____ her first book?

4 How old _____ left the boy band?

2 Choosing the correct tense

Tick (✔) the correct form of the verb.

The life of David Hockney

1 David Hockney _____ in 1937 in Bradford, a town in the north of England.
- [ ] born
- [ ] is born
- [ ] was born

2 He _____ interested in painting and design all his life.
- [ ] is
- [ ] was
- [ ] has been

3 He _____ at the Royal College of Art from 1959–62.
- [ ] studies
- [ ] has studied
- [ ] studied

4 Over the past twenty years, he _____ to most parts of the world.
- [ ] has travelled
- [ ] travels
- [ ] travelled

5 He first _____ to America when he was twenty-five.
- [ ] went
- [ ] has gone
- [ ] has been

6 His most famous work is called *A Bigger Splash*, which _____ in 1967.
- [ ] painted
- [ ] has painted
- [ ] was painted

7 Hockney _____ stage sets and books.
- [ ] also designed
- [ ] has also designed
- [ ] is also designed

8 He _____ in Los Angeles for many years.
- [ ] lives
- [ ] has lived
- [ ] lived

9 He _____ married.
- [ ] never
- [ ] has never
- [ ] is never

10 He _____ with friends in a villa in the mountains above Los Angeles.
- [ ] lives
- [ ] has lived
- [ ] lived

3 Conversations

T 7.1 Write the conversations using the cues.

1 A You / be / brown! Where / you / be?

<u>You're brown! Where have you been?</u>

B We / be / on holiday.

_____

A Where / you / go?

_____

B We / go / Spain.

_____

A When / you / get back?

_____

B Last night. The plane / land / 6.00 in the evening.

_____

2 A What / you / do / to your finger?

_____

B I / cut / myself.

_____

A How / you / do that?

_____

B I / cook / and the knife / slip.

_____

A you / put / anything on it?

_____

B No. It's not that bad.

4 *been* or *gone*?

Complete the sentences with *been* or *gone*.

1 **A** Where's Mum?

    B She's _____ to the post office.

2 Where have you _____ ? You're so late!

3 **A** Are you going to the library today?

    B No, I've already _____ . I went yesterday.

4 If anyone phones, tell them I've _____ to lunch.
    I'll be back at two.

5 We've never _____ to Japan, but we'd like to go.

6 **A** When are you going on holiday?

    B We've already _____ . We went to Florida.

7 **A** What happened to your neighbours?

    B Didn't you know? They've _____ to live in
    the south of France.

5 Time expressions

1 Do the time expression and the verb go
together (✔) or not (✗)?

	Past Simple	Present Perfect
1 for	✔	✔
2 since	✗	✔
3 in (1960)		
4 ago		
5 at (two o'clock)		
6 just		
7 before		
8 yet		
9 already		
10 never		

2 Put the word in brackets in the correct place in
the sentences.

1 I've heard about your accident. (just)

    _____

2 Have you had breakfast? (yet)

    _____

3 I've finished my exams. (already)

    _____

4 Have you been to Thailand? (ever)

    _____

5 I haven't seen that film. (yet)

    _____

3 Write sentences for the situations with the verb in brackets
and *just*, *already*, or *yet*.

1 You're having a salad in a café. You stop eating for a
minute and the waiter tries to take your plate away.

    You say: Excuse me! _____

    _____ . (not finish)

2 You had a cup of coffee. Your sister comes in and offers
you another cup.

    You say: No, thanks. _____

    _____ . (have one)

3 Henri went out two minutes ago. The phone rings.
It's someone for Henri.

    You say: _____ . (go out)

4 You rush home to see the World Cup final on TV.
You want to know if you've missed the beginning.

    You ask: _____ ? (start)

5 You're doing your homework. Your friend calls round to
invite you out for the evening.

    You say: _____ . (not do)

6 You fed the cat at eight o'clock. At nine o'clock, your
sister starts to feed the cat again.

    You say: _____ . (feed her)

6 Talking about you

T 7.2 Answer the questions about you.

1 Have you been shopping recently?

_____

2 What did you buy?

_____

3 How much have you spent today?

_____

4 Have you had a busy day?

_____

5 Have you seen any good films recently?

_____

_____

6 What lessons have you had today?

_____

_____

7 Correcting mistakes

Correct the mistakes in these sentences.

1 How long do you know the teacher?

_____

_____

2 This is the first time I eat Thai food.

_____

_____

3 What have you done last night?

_____

_____

4 I study English for four years.

_____

_____

5 When have you got your hair cut?

_____

_____

6 I have seen Peter yesterday.

_____

_____

Tense review

8 Curriculum vitae

1 T 7.3 Read Stella's curriculum vitae. Then complete the job interview below.

I Where do you live ?

S In Newton, near Swansea.

I _____ you _____ to university?

S Yes, I have. I _____ to Bristol University from 1995 to 1998.

I What subjects _____ ?

S _____ and _____ .

I _____ any languages?

S Yes, I do. I _____ fluently.

I _____ you ever _____ in Spain?

S Yes, I _____ . I _____ and _____ in Barcelona for a year.

I What kind of work _____ you _____ there?

S I _____ .

I What _____ now?

S I _____ near Exeter.

I How long _____ there?

S Since _____ .

2 Complete the sentences. Use the Present Simple, the Past Simple, or the Present Perfect.

1 She _____ in the village of Newton near Swansea.

2 She _____ Music and Sociology at university.

3 She _____ Spanish when she _____ in Barcelona.

4 She _____ in a children's hospital since April 1998.

5 She _____ climbing and going to the cinema in her free time.

6 When she was at school she _____ in a music shop at weekends.

CURRICULUM VITAE

Name   Stella Ann Marcham
Address   78 Bryn Lane
            Newton
            Swansea
            South Wales
            SA3 5DL
Telephone   01792 34651
Date of birth   15 September 1976

Education

1985–1994	Kingsmead School, Swansea
1995–1998	Bristol University
	BA (Hons) Music and Sociology
Languages	Fluent Spanish
Computing skills	Microsoft Word, Excel

Work experience

April 1998–present	Music therapist at Ferndale Children's Hospital in Roundhay, near Exeter.
1996–1997	Secretary of the university climbing club. Led a team to the Alps.
July 1994–May 1995	Lived in Barcelona. Worked as an English assistant in a junior school. Acquired excellent Spanish language skills.
October 1992–June 1994	Worked at weekends in a music shop.

Interests

Travel, cinema, working with children, climbing.

Present Perfect passive

9 Active or passive?

Choose the correct form of the verb in these sentences.

1 Angela *'s just promoted* / *'s just been promoted* to area manager of Eastern Europe.
2 I *'ve applied* / *'ve been applied* for a job.
3 How many times *have you injured* / *have you been injured* playing football?
4 Bob's wife *has just lost* / *has just been lost* her job.
5 My sister *has passed* / *has been passed* her final exams.
6 My brother *has given* / *has been given* tickets to the concert.
7 The population of our city *has risen* / *has been risen* to nearly a million.
8 A strike *has called* / *has been called* by the air traffic controllers.
9 They *haven't offered* / *haven't been offered* more money by the management.
10 How much money *have you saved* / *have you been saved* for your round-the-world trip?

10 Two newspaper stories

1 Complete the newspaper stories with the correct form of the verbs in brackets. Use the Present Perfect or Past Simple, active or passive.

The Loch Ness Wallet

Fourteen years ago Spanish tourist Gaspar Sanchez (1) _____ (drop) his wallet into the waters of Loch Ness in Scotland. His passport, his car keys, his business card, and his money (2) _____ (lose) in 150m of water. This week the phone (3) _____ (ring) in Señor Sanchez's Barcelona flat and a Scottish policeman told him, 'Sir, your wallet (4) _____ (find)!

It (5) _____ (discover) last Sunday on the bed of the loch by some scientists in a submarine looking for the Loch Ness monster!'

◆ ◆ ◆

Señor Sanchez said, 'The whole thing is absolutely amazing. Apparently my wallet and its contents (6) _____ (put) in the post to me already. I should get them tomorrow. I can't believe it!'

Picassos taken in €60m raid

Swedish police (7) _____ just _____ (announce) that five paintings by Picasso (8) _____ (steal) from the Museum of Modern Art in Stockholm.

The paintings (9) _____ (value) by experts at 60 million euros.

Police believe that they (10) _____ (take) early on Saturday evening, but for some reason the museum's burglar alarm (11) _____ (not go off) and the theft (12) _____ (not discover) until Monday morning. No clues (13) _____ so far _____ (find) at the scene of the crime.

2 Write the questions. Use the information in the newspaper stories.

1 **When did Gaspar Sanchez lose his wallet?**
   Fourteen years ago.

2 _____?
   Last Sunday.

3 _____?
   Five paintings by Picasso.

4 _____?
   Yes, they have. At 60 million euros.

5 _____?
   Saturday evening.

6 _____?
   No, none. Not yet.

Vocabulary

11 Words with more than one meaning

1 Look at the dictionary entry for *course*. How many meanings do you know?

★ **course** /kɔːs/ **noun 1** [C] **a course (in/on sth)** a complete series of lessons: *I've enrolled on an English course.* • *A course in self-defence.* **2** [C] one of the parts of a meal: *a three-course lunch* • *I had chicken for the main course.* **3** [C] an area where golf is played or where certain types of race take place: *a golf course* • *a racecourse* **4** [C] **a course (of sth)** a series of medical treatments: *the doctor put her on a course of radiation therapy.* **5** [C, U] the route or direction that sth, especially an aeroplane, ship, or river takes: *We changed course and sailed toward land.* • to be on/off course (= going in the right/wrong direction) (figurative) *I'm on course* (= making the right amount of progress) *to finish this work by the end of the week.*

2 In these sentences the words in *italics* have more than one meaning. What is the correct definition here? Find one other meaning. Use your dictionary if necessary.

1 You've got a dirty *mark* on your shirt. Did you spill your food?
2 How many political *parties* are there in your country?
3 Everyone has the *right* to live in peace.
4 The *train* leaves from platform 5.
5 You gave her ten pounds, but you only gave me five. That's not *fair*!
6 It was *mean* of him not to invite you to his party.
7 I'll put the picture up if you give me a hammer and a *nail*.
8 Who holds the world *record* for the high jump?
9 It's common to *tip* waiters and taxi drivers ten per cent.
10 My brother works for a law *firm*.

Pronunciation

12 Word stress

T 7.4 Put the words in the box in the correct columns.

business	degree	absolutely
applicant	Argentina	behaviour
competition	discover	editor
experience	fluent	foreign
interesting	interpreter	Japan
journalist	political	publication
resign	pollution	career

A ••	B ••	C •••
business	*degree*	___
___	___	___
___	___	___

D •••	E ••••	F ••••
___	___	___
___	___	___
___	___	___
	___	

Prepositions

13 Noun + preposition

Complete the sentences with a preposition from the box. Some are used more than once.

with	for	between	on	to
out of	in	of	about	

1 I had a crash this morning. Fortunately I didn't do much damage **to** my car.
2 Ari isn't here this week. He's _____ holiday.
3 We're _____ coffee. Could you go to the shop and get some?
4 This morning I got a cheque in the post _____ 100 euros.
5 You're really annoying me. You're doing it _____ purpose, aren't you?
6 Can you tell the difference _____ butter and margarine?
7 There have been a lot of complaints _____ your behaviour.
8 The trouble _____ you is that you don't listen to anybody.
9 I'm tired of cooking. Let's eat out _____ a change.
10 How much do you spend a week _____ average?
11 Be careful when you talk to the boss. He's _____ a terrible mood today.
12 Have you got any photos _____ your girlfriend?

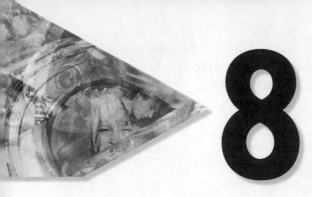

8

Conditionals
Time clauses • Money
Phrasal verbs – phrasal verbs with more than one meaning

Just imagine!

Conditionals 1 and time clauses

1 Matching

Match a line in **A** with a line in **B** and a line in **C**.

A	B	C
1 If you go to Paris,	we'll be late for school.	She might not be home until 9.00.
2 If we can afford it,	go inside the shop.	The views are fantastic.
3 If I don't hear from you today,	tell him I never want to see him again.	The one we have now is very unreliable.
4 If the music is too loud,	we'll buy a new car soon.	I don't mind.
5 If we don't leave soon,	she'll phone you from the office.	It'll be the second time this week.
6 If there's nothing interesting in the window,	you can turn down the radio.	He really hurt my feelings.
7 If she has to work late,	you must go to the top of the Eiffel Tower.	I need to talk to you about something.
8 If Daniel rings,	I'll phone you tomorrow.	You might find something you like.

2 Conversations

T 8.1 Here are two conversations mixed up. Tom and Lisa are talking about shopping, and Jody and Pete are planning a barbecue. Match the lines with the correct person and put them in order.

Shopping

4	Tom
	Lisa
	Tom
	Lisa
	Tom
	Lisa
	Tom
	Lisa
	Tom

1 That's a good idea. Let's do that.
2 OK. If I see some, I'll get them for you. What colour do you want?
3 I want them to match my coat, so they should be dark brown.
4 I'm going to the shops. Do you want anything?
5 Erm … I'll try to find a pair of dark brown gloves, but I'm not very good with colours.
6 OK. I'll make an apple pie.
7 No, I don't think so. Oh, hang on. I need some warm gloves.
8 She likes most things, I think. Meat, fish …
9 OK. I won't.
10 And another thing. Could you get some stamps?
11 If I do the main course, will you do the dessert?
12 What shall we make for dinner when your sister comes? What does she eat?
13 Don't worry. If you're not sure, don't buy them.
14 If the weather's good, we could have a barbecue.
15 OK. I'll get two books of first-class stamps.
16 And I'll do hamburgers and some green salad.

Barbecue

12	Jody
	Pete
	Jody
	Pete
	Jody
	Pete
	Jody

3 Zero conditional

Complete the sentences with some advice.

1 If you have a headache, **take some aspirin.**

2 If you can't get to sleep, _____

_____

3 If you get sunburned, _____

_____

4 If you want to stop smoking, _____

_____

5 If you have a problem at school, _____

_____

6 If you can't wake up in the mornings, _____

_____

4 Time clauses

1 Combine the sentences with the time expressions in brackets. Use the Present Simple.

1 I'll cook supper. I'll come home. (as soon as)
   I'll cook supper as soon as I come home.

2 I want to finish my work. We're going out. (before)

_____

3 She's going to look after the cat. I'll be away on holiday. (while)

_____

4 I'll email you. I'll arrive. (as soon as)

_____

5 We'll find a hotel. We'll arrive in Paris. (when)

_____

6 She won't speak to him. He'll say sorry. (until)

_____

7 Drink your coffee. It'll get cold. (before)

_____

8 Don't cross the road. You'll see the green man. (until)

_____

9 I'll give you a ring. We'll get back from holiday. (after)

_____

10 Are you going to stay with Paola? You'll be in Italy. (while)

2 Choose the time expression which best completes the sentence.

1 *Before / If / When* we get to our holiday resort, we'll send you a postcard.

2 Don't worry, we won't get lost. But *if / until / when* we do, we'll call you on our mobile.

3 Laura, please wash the dishes *until / after / while* you've finished your meal.

4 *As soon as / If / Before* we get to London, we'll go straight to see Big Ben and the Houses of Parliament.

5 Could you please get your hair cut *while / before / until* you go to your sister's wedding?

6 My darling, I'll love you *until / when / as soon as* I die.

7 *Before / Until / As soon as* you've finished your homework, you can go out with your friends.

8 *Until / If / Before* you find out Emma's exam results, will you please let me know?

9 I'm not going to the party on my own. I'll wait *before / until / when* you get home.

10 You tidy the garage *while / as soon as / until* I wash the car. That'll be quickest.

11 I'll come round to your house *after / while / before* I've finished my piano practice.

12 Can you wake me up *when / if / before* you get up tomorrow morning?

13 *If / As soon as / Until* they offer me the job, I'll take it. But I don't think they will.

Conditionals 2

5 Second conditional

T 8.2 Rewrite the sentences with the second conditional.

1 I can't take you to the airport because I haven't got a car.
If I had a car I could take you to the airport.

2 I've got a headache. I'm not going swimming.

_____

3 I don't know the answer, so I can't tell you.

_____

4 We won't have a holiday this year because we haven't got
any money.

_____

5 I haven't got any spare time so I won't learn Russian.

_____

6 We haven't got a big house. We can't invite friends to stay.

_____

7 There aren't any eggs, so I won't make a cake.

_____

8 I'm not very clever, so I won't be a doctor.

_____

9 I haven't got a mobile, so you can't call me.

_____

10 He can't win the lottery. He never buys a ticket.

_____

11 Francis works very hard. He has no time to spend with
his family.

_____

12 We've got three children, so we won't take a year off and
travel the world.

_____

6 First or second conditional?

Complete the sentences with the correct
form of the verb in brackets.

1 If it _____ (rain) this weekend,
we _____ (not be able) to
play tennis.

2 Give me Anika's letter. If I _____
(pass) a letter box, I _____ (post)
it for you.

3 I work about 80 hours a week, so I'm
very busy. If I _____ (have) any spare
time, I _____ (take up) a sport
like golf.

4 If I _____ (be) taller and thinner, I
_____ (can) be a model!

5 Please start your meal. If you _____
(not have) your soup now, it _____
(go) cold.

6 **A** I think we have a mouse in the kitchen.
B If you _____ (have) a cat, it
_____ soon _____ (disappear).

7 If you _____ (need) any help, let me
know and I _____ (come) and help
you straight away.

8 You're a brilliant cook! If I _____
(can) cook as well as you, I _____
(open) a restaurant.

9 If there _____ (be) any tickets left for
the concert, _____ you _____
(buy) two for me and Tom?

10 What noisy neighbours you've got! If my
neighbours _____ (be) as bad as
yours, I _____ (go) crazy.

7 Correcting mistakes

Correct the mistakes in these sentences.

1 I'll make some tea when everyone will arrive.
   I'll make some tea when everyone arrives.

2 If I could go anywhere in the world, I'll go to Fiji.

_____

_____

3 If I'll see Jane, I'll tell her to phone you.

_____

_____

4 If I have lots of money, I'd buy an aeroplane.

_____

_____

5 When I'll go back to university, I'll email you.

_____

_____

6 If you would know my brother, you'd know what I mean!

_____

_____

7 If you would come from my town, you would recognize the street names.

_____

_____

8 If you don't be careful, you'll lose your bag.

_____

_____

8 I'd rather ...

> ❗ *I'd rather* (= I would rather) + infinitive means the same as *I'd prefer to*.
> I don't like studying. **I'd rather be** outside playing tennis.

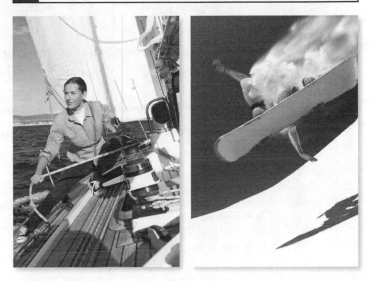

Say what you would rather do in these situations.

1 If you had to choose between going snowboarding or going sailing, which would you choose?
   I'd rather go _____

2 If you're thirsty, would you rather have a coffee or a cold drink?

   _____

3 If you could choose between travelling by plane or by train, which would you rather do?

   _____

4 You have to choose between fizzy mineral water or still mineral water.

   _____

5 What do you want to watch on TV, the news or a quiz show?

   _____

6 Which would you rather have as a pet, a cat or a dog?

   _____

7 If you had to choose between being rich or being famous, which would you choose?

   _____

8 In a restaurant you have to choose between boiled potatoes and french fries.

Vocabulary

9 Money

1 Put the words from the box in the correct columns. Some words can go in more than one place.

currency	wealthy	safe	broke
accountant	bankrupt	waste	win
millionaire	economy	earn	save
cash machine	credit card	loan	will
windfall	economic	salary	bet
penniless	savings	invest	coins
spending spree	cashier	wages	cheque
economical	fortune		

Noun	Verb	Adjective
loan	loan	broke

2 Choose the correct words.

1 My aunt keeps all her money in a *cash dispenser* / *safe* under her bed.

2 I'm *bankrupt* / *broke*. Can you lend me ten pounds until the weekend?

3 The president said that the *economic* / *economical* situation was very serious.

4 She has *wasted* / *invested* all her money in government bonds.

5 What's the *coin* / *currency* of India?

6 My uncle's *an accountant* / *a millionaire*, he helps me look after my finances.

7 There's a *cash machine* / *credit card* at the bank if you need money.

8 I like horse racing, but I never *bet* / *win* any money. I think gambling is stupid.

9 Alan's parents are *penniless* / *wealthy*. They've just bought him a car.

10 My *salary is* / *wages are* paid into my bank account every month.

11 When my grandfather died, I found he left me some money in his *will* / *savings*.

Pronunciation

10 Ways of pronouncing *oo*

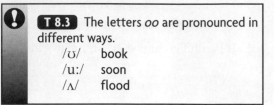

T 8.3 The letters *oo* are pronounced in different ways.
/ʊ/   book
/u:/ soon
/ʌ/   flood

T 8.4 Put the words in *italics* in the correct column, **A**, **B**, or **C**.

1 Have you read the '*Good Food*' guide to London?

2 The best *cooks* use a *wooden spoon* to stir the sauce.

3 *Look!* There's a *pool* of *blood* on the carpet!

4 If I won the *football pools*, I'd be *flooded* with begging letters.

5 We *foolishly booked* a *room* at the hotel without asking the price.

6 I wear a *woollen* sweater when it's *cool*.

7 He *stood* on a *stool* and climbed onto the *roof*.

A	B	C
/ʊ/ **book**	/u:/ **soon**	/ʌ/ **flood**
<u>good</u>	<u>food</u>	_____
_____	_____	_____
_____	_____	_____
_____	_____	_____
_____	_____	_____
_____	_____	_____
	_____	
	_____	

11 Ways of pronouncing *ou*

> ⓘ **T 8.5** The letters *ou* are also pronounced in many different ways. For example:
> /ɔː/   four
> /uː/   group

1 **T 8.6** <u>Underline</u> the word with the different pronunciation.

	1	2	3	4
1	would	should	<u>shoulder</u>	could
2	your	sour	court	pour
3	accountant	country	count	fountain
4	though	ought	bought	thought
5	enough	tough	rough	cough
6	anonymous	mouse	enormous	furious
7	trouble	double	doubt	country
8	through	group	though	soup

2 **T 8.7** Transcribe the words in phonetic script.

1 It's the /θɔːt/ _____ that /kaʊnts/
_____ .

2 There's an /ɪˈnɔːməs/ _____ /maʊs/
_____ in the kitchen.

3 I have no /daʊt/ _____ that my boss
will be /ˈfjʊəriəs/ _____ .

4 You /ɔːt/ _____ to do something about
that /kɒf/_____ .

5 I have a lot of /ˈtrʌbl/ _____ with
noisy /ˈneɪbəz/ _____ .

Phrasal verbs

12 Phrasal verbs with more than one meaning
Rewrite the sentences with a phrasal verb from the box in place of the words in *italics*. Careful! Each verb is used twice with a different meaning.

make up	get over	hang on
work out	put out	go on

1 I'm trying to *calculate* how much you owe me.
I'm trying to work out how much you owe me.

2 She goes to the gym twice a week to *exercise*.

_____

3 **A** Can I speak to Martin?
   B *Wait a moment.* I'll go and get him.
   B _____ . I'll go and get him.

4 *Hold on tight!* We're going to crash into the car in front!

_____

5 Can you hear all that noise outside? I wonder what's *happening*.

_____

6 **A** Are you listening to me?'
   B Yes, of course, dear. *Continue speaking.* I'm listening to every word.'
   B _____

7 The police *publicly announced* a warning about the escaped prisoner.

_____

8 If you want a sweet, *extend* your hand and I'll give you one.

_____

9 How are we going to *climb over* the wall?

_____

10 He's really angry now, but he'll *recover from* it.

_____

11 Is that a true story, or did you *invent it*?

_____

12 Do you want to come with me or not? You've got to *decide*.

_____ your mind.

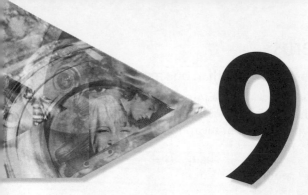

9

Modal verbs 2 – Probability
Continuous infinitive • Word formation
Prepositions – adjective + preposition

Relationships

Modal verbs of probability in the present

1 Matching

Match a line in **A** with a line in **B**.

A	**B**
1 She can't enjoy skydiving. _e_	a She can't stand him.
2 You can't be hungry ___	b It's already after midnight.
3 She must be out. ___	c She gave him a huge hug when he walked in.
4 He can't be English ___	d She isn't answering the phone.
5 You must be very pleased ___	e It's so dangerous!
6 They must be tired. ___	f I'm not going to jump out of a plane!
7 They must know each other well. ___	g with your excellent exam results.
8 He can't be coming tonight. ___	h after such a huge meal.
9 You must be joking! ___	i They've been travelling all night.
10 They can't be getting married! ___	j with a name like Heinrich.

2 Why is he late?

1 Enrique is always on time for class but today he is late. Suggest reasons using *must*, *might*, *could*, or *may*.

1 Is he still asleep? (might)

He might still be asleep.

2 Is he ill? (must)

_____

3 Is he in the coffee bar? (might)

_____

4 Does he have a doctor's appointment? (could)

_____

5 Is he stuck in a traffic jam? (may)

_____

6 Is his bus late? (might)

_____

7 Does he want to miss the test? (must)

_____

2 Rewrite the sentences in exercise 1 with *can't*. Then give a reason.

1 **He can't still be asleep because he always gets up very early.**

2 _____
_____

3 _____
_____

4 _____
_____

5 _____
_____

6 _____
_____

7 _____
_____

3 The continuous infinitive

> **!** 1 The continuous infinitive is used after a modal verb of probability to express a possible activity in progress at the moment.
> His office light's on. He must **be working** late.
> It's only 9.10. They can't **be having** a break yet.

T 9.1 Complete the conversations with suitable verbs in the continuous infinitive.

1 **A** Do you know where Ben is?

B I'm not sure. He may **be playing** games on the computer.

2 **A** Where's Birgit?

B She's upstairs. She must _____ to music in her room.

A She's not in her room.

B Try the bathroom. She might _____ a shower.

3 **A** I can't find the thing that changes the TV channel.

B The remote control? Stand up. You could _____ on it.

4 **A** Have you seen the newspaper?

B I think James picked it up. He may _____ it.

5 **A** What's that noise?

B It sounds like an ambulance. They must _____ someone to hospital.

6 **A** Look over there! It's Kate and Alex.

B She can't _____ his hand. She doesn't like him.

A They must _____ out together. I don't believe it!

7 **A** What's happening outside?

B It sounds like workmen. They must _____ up the road outside.

A What for?

B I don't know. They could _____ a broken water pipe.

Modal verbs of probability in the past

4 must have, might have, may have

Look at the pictures. What must have happened? What might have happened? Write sentences.

1 <u>He must have locked himself out.</u>

<u>He might have lost his key.</u>

2 _____

_____

3 _____

_____

4 _____

_____

5 _____

_____

6 _____

_____

5 Changing sentences

Rewrite these sentences using the modal verb in brackets.

1 I'm sure she's had a holiday. (must)

   <u>She must have had a holiday.</u>

2 I'm sure you didn't work hard for your exams. (can't)

   _____

3 I think they've gone to the station. (could)

   _____

4 Perhaps I left my mobile in the Internet café. (might)

   _____

5 I'm sure he hasn't bought another new car. (can't)

   _____

6 He has probably been on a diet. (must)

   _____

7 It's possible that they got married in secret. (could)

   _____

8 Perhaps he called while we were out. (may)

   _____

6 A poem

1 **T 9.2** Read the poem.

The house is not the same since you left

The house is not the same since you left
the cooker is angry – it blames me

The TV tries desperately to stay busy

but occasionally I catch it staring out of the window

The washing-up's feeling sorry for itself again

it just sits there saying

'What's the point, what's the point?'

The curtains count the days

Nothing in the house will talk to me

I think your armchair's dead

The kettle tried to comfort me at first

but you know what its attention span is like

I've not told the plants yet

they think you're still on holiday

The bathroom misses you

I hardly see it these days

It still can't believe you didn't take it with you

The bedroom won't even look at me

since you left it keeps its eyes closed

all it wants to do is sleep, remembering better times

trying to lose itself in dreams

it seems like it's taken the easy way out

but at night I hear the pillows

weeping into the sheets.

Henry Normal

2 Are the statements possible (✓) or impossible (✗)?
Write (?) if you are not sure.

1 ☒ He must have left her.
   ☑ She must have left him.

2 ☐ They can't have been husband and wife.
   ☐ They definitely lived together.

3 ☐ They must have been together for a long time.
   ☐ They can't have been together for a long time.

4 ☐ He might be glad she's gone.
   ☐ He must be missing her very much.

5 ☐ The house must seem very quiet.
   ☐ He might have pets to keep him company.

6 ☐ He must have done something to upset her.
   ☐ She has definitely done something to upset him.

7 ☐ He can't be using the bathroom much.
   ☐ He might be trying to avoid using the bathroom.

8 ☐ She must have spent a lot of time in the bathroom.
   ☐ The bathroom might have been her favourite room.

9 ☐ He might be sleeping downstairs.
   ☐ He can't be sleeping in their old bedroom.

Vocabulary

7 Word formation

1 Complete the chart. Make nouns from the character adjectives using the suffixes in the box. Use your dictionary if necessary.

> -n   -ism   -ness   -ity

Adjective	Noun
shy	_____
optimistic	_____
reliable	_____
ambitious	_____
lazy	_____
pessimistic	_____
generous	_____
tidy	_____
moody	_____
sensitive	_____

2 Complete the sentences using words from exercise 1.

1 Karen's really _____ these days. You never know if she's going to be cheerful or bad-tempered.

2 My best friend suffered from terrible _____ at school. She went red every time somebody spoke to her.

3 I'm surprised she was late for the meeting. She's normally so _____ .

4 He doesn't show much _____ . I think he's more interested in having a good time than getting a better job.

5 I tried to apologize to Anna after the argument, but I'm not _____ that we'll ever be best friends again.

6 Look at the fabulous present Hiro gave me. I can't believe his _____ !

7 Are you sure you want to share a flat with Nicole? You're so messy, but she's famous for her _____ .

8 Get up off that sofa and help me with the preparations for your party! Your _____ is really beginning to annoy me.

Pronunciation

8 Connected speech

⚠ **T 9.3** Notice how the consonant sounds are linked to the vowel sounds that follow:

He must‿have‿eaten‿all‿of‿Ann's‿oranges.
She can't‿have‿asked‿Al's‿aunt.

1 **T 9.4** Mark the linked words in these sentences.

1 She must have eaten the cheese.

2 You can't have seen him.

3 He can't have arrived early.

4 He might have gone out for a cup of coffee.

5 She might have been angry.

6 They can't have been in love.

7 They might have written it down.

8 He must have been to Africa.

2 **T 9.5** Say these sentences in phonetic script aloud. Notice the linked words.

1 /hiː kʊd əv gɒn əbrɔːd/

2 /ðeɪ maɪt əv iːtən ɪt ɔːl/

3 /ʃiː meɪ bi əraɪvɪŋ ðis iːvnɪŋ/

4 /ðeɪ məs bi kʌmɪŋ suːn/

5 /ðeɪ kɑːnt nəʊ hɪm ət ɔːl/

9 Shifting stress

T 9.6 Read the conversations. Circle the words that **B** stressed.

1 **A** Mr Harper must have left the black bag in the taxi.

  B Did you say Mr Harper must have left the (blue) bag in the taxi?

2 **A** Mr Harper must have left the black bag in the taxi.

  B Did you say Mr Harper must have left the black (suitcase) in the taxi?

3 **A** Mr Harper must have left the black bag in the taxi.

  B Did you say Mrs Harper must have left the black bag in the taxi?

4 **A** Mr Harper must have left the black bag in the taxi.

  B Did you say Mr Harper must have put the black bag in the taxi?

5 **A** Mr Harper must have left the black bag in the taxi.

  B Did you say Mr Harper must have left the black bag in the train?

6 **A** Mr Harper must have left the black bag in the taxi.

  B Did you say Mr Harper must have left a black bag in the taxi?

7 **A** Mr Harper must have left the black bag in the taxi.

  B Did you say Mr Harper might have left the black bag in the taxi?

8 **A** Mr Harper must have left the black bag in the taxi.

  B Did you say Mr Harper can't have left the black bag in the taxi?

Prepositions

10 Adjective + preposition

Complete the sentences with a preposition from the box.

for	at	about	with
to	in	of	from

1 Thailand is famous **for** its temples and beaches.

2 **A** I'm very angry _____ you.

  B Why? What have I done?

3 Are you any good _____ maths? I'm hopeless.

4 Jenny's getting married _____ Matt. Did you know?

5 My sister's very different _____ me. I'm blonde but she's brunette.

6 I haven't heard from my brother for ages. I'm a bit worried _____ him.

7 I'm tired _____ painting this wall. I need a break.

8 I feel very sorry _____ Jenny. She's had a lot of bad luck recently.

9 Teenagers are often rude _____ their parents.

10 You passed your exams! I'm so proud _____ you.

11 Some children like to keep a light on at night because they're afraid _____ the dark.

12 Many dentists say that chewing sugar-free gum is good _____ your teeth.

13 Bill is good-looking, witty and charming. I'm very jealous _____ him!

14 **A** I told her I thought she was stupid.

  B That wasn't very kind _____ you.

15 Are you interested _____ going to the cinema tonight? There's a good film on.

16 His email was full _____ spelling mistakes. He should be more careful when he types.

17 **A** What are you so excited _____ ?

  B We're going on holiday tomorrow!

18 **A** The train leaves at eight o'clock.

  B Are you sure _____ that?

19 When you leave home, you're responsible _____ everything!

20 I'm fed up _____ this weather! Where's the sunshine gone?

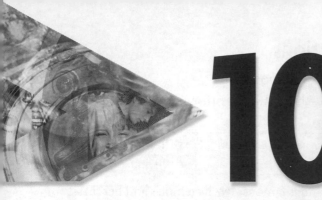

10

Present Perfect Continuous • Time expressions
Suffixes • Prepositions of time

Obsessions

Present Perfect Continuous

1 Present Perfect Simple or Continuous?

1 **T 10.1** Underline the correct form of the verb.

1 I've *had* / *been having* an accident with your car, Helen. I'm really sorry.

2 I don't believe it! Somebody has *eaten* / *been eating* my chocolates! They've nearly all gone!

3 I've *waited* / *been waiting* for you for ages! Where have you been?

4 I've *broken* / *been breaking* a glass. I'm awfully sorry.

5 How many biscuits have you *eaten* / *been eating* today?

6 **A** Why is your face so red?
  B I've *run* / *been running*.

7 I have never *met* / *been meeting* a nicer person in my life.

8 How long have you *known* / *been knowing* Charles and Lisa?

9 He's *written* / *been writing* a book for nearly a year. It'll be finished soon.

10 He's *written* / *been writing* a book. I saw it in the bookshop.

11 The children are very quiet. They've *watched* / *been watching* videos all morning.

12 They've *watched* / *been watching* five videos already.

2 Complete the sentences with the correct form of the verb in brackets, Present Perfect Simple or Continuous.

1 I'm exhausted! I **'ve been working** (work) all day, and I **haven't finished** (not finish) yet.

2 He _____ (have) a lot of jobs over the past few years.

3 Someone _____ (move) my car keys. I _____ (look) for them for ages, but I _____ (not find) them yet.

4 I _____ (shop) all morning, but I _____ (not buy) anything.

5 That's one of the best jokes I _____ ever _____ (hear).

6 **A** You're really dirty! What _____ you _____ (do)?
  B I _____ (work) in the garden.

7 Everything's white! It _____ (snow).

8 I _____ (listen) to you for the past half an hour, but I'm afraid I _____ (not understand) a single word.

9 **A** Are you all right?
  B No, I _____ (work) on the computer for hours, and I've got a headache.

10 I _____ (try) to lose weight for ages. I _____ (lose) five kilos so far.

2 Replying with questions

Complete the questions.

1 **A** Raoul is a singer in a band.

 B How long *has he been a singer?*

 How many records *has he made?*

2 **A** I'm learning to drive.

 B How long _____ ?

 _____ bought a car yet?

3 **A** Jamal is a teacher.

 B How long _____ ?

 How many schools _____ ?

4 **A** At last! You said you'd be here ages ago.

 B I'm sorry. How long _____ ?

5 **A** Joey is getting married to Andy next week.

 B How many _____ invited to the wedding?

 How long _____ known Andy?

6 **A** What a surprise! I haven't seen you for years.

 What _____ doing all this time?

 B I've been abroad, actually.

 A Where _____ been?

7 **A** Freya has been to the States several times.

 B How many times _____ ?

8 **A** I'm moving to Mexico in a few months.

 B Have you _____ to learn Spanish yet?

9 **A** My grandmother is on holiday at the moment.

 B Where _____ ?

10 **A** She always goes to France for her holidays.

 B How many years _____ ?

Simple and Continuous revision

3 Matching

Match a line in **A** with a line in **B**.

A	B
1 I think _a_ I'm thinking _b_	a you're beautiful. b of moving to New York.
2 I get the bus to work. ___ I'm getting the bus to work today. ___	a My car's broken down. b It's difficult to park near my office.
3 She might study ___ She might be studying ___	a German when she goes to university. b in her room. The light's on.
4 He has ___ He's having ___	a a difficult time at work. b a very big family.
5 She cut ___ She was cutting ___	a her foot on a broken bottle. b the grass when it started to rain.
6 She must be washing ___ She must wash ___	a her hair. I can hear the water running. b her hair every single day!
7 I've written ___ I've been writing ___	a this letter since lunchtime. b three letters today.
8 Misha's gone ___ Misha's been going ___	a out with Anya for ages. b to Russia to see his family.

4 Simple or Continuous?

Complete the sentences with the correct form of the verb in brackets, Simple or Continuous. Look at the verb form or tense at the end for help.

1 We **were doing** (do) the washing-up when Julia **phoned** (phone). **Past**

2 Julia _____ (come) from Wales. **Present (all time)**

3 She _____ (come) to see us tomorrow. **Future arrangement**

4 She _____ (work) for an advertising company. **Present (all time)**

5 She _____ (work) for the same company for a year. **Present Perfect**

6 She _____ (have) the same boss for six months. **Present Perfect**

7 She _____ (have) a row with her boss again yesterday. **Past**

8 So now Helen _____ (want) to change her job. **Present**

9 She _____ (think) of working abroad. **Present**

10 Her parents _____ (not think) this is a good idea. **Present**

11 She'd like _____ (find) a job in the tourist industry. **Infinitive**

12 She should _____ (work) now, but she isn't. She's daydreaming. **Infinitive**

13 She _____ (go) to bed very late last night. **Past**

14 When she _____ (wake) up this morning, it _____ (rain). **Past**

15 She _____ (take) some aspirin now because she _____ (have) a headache. **Present**

16 She wants _____ (go) home. **Infinitive**

17 If she were at home, she would _____ (sit) in her kitchen having a cup of coffee. **Infinitive**

Time expressions

5 When Richard met Heather

Look at the information about Richard and Heather. Complete the questions and answers.

Richard

age 0	Born 1975 in Oxford, England
11	Went to Cherwell School for six years
18	Went to Bath University for three years
19	Started going out with Helena
22	Went to work in Madrid Feb–July 1997
23	Broke up with Helena, Christmas 1998 Met Heather at a party
24	Got a job in a bookshop
25	Married Heather 23 March 2001. Promoted to manager of the bookshop, autumn 2002
26 now	Bought a house in Woodstock

Heather

0	Born 1972 in Melbourne, Australia
11	Joined a drama group. Start of a life-long passion
18	Came to live in Britain, summer 1990
19	Trained as a drama teacher for three years
23	Taught in Hungary for two years
24	Met and married Harry August 1996
25	Had a daughter, Joanne, born 13 May 1997
26	Came back to Britain with Joanne but without Harry 1997
now	Divorced Harry Started teaching in a school in Oxford Sept 1998. Met Richard Christmas 1998

1. When _____? In 1975.

2. How long _____ at Cherwell School? Until _____.

3. How long _____? Three years.

4. How long _____ Helena? For _____.

5. How long _____ in Madrid? _____.

6. Where _____? At a party.

7. How long _____ in the bookshop? Since _____.

8. How long _____ manager? Since _____.

9. When _____? _____ 23 March 2001.

10. How long _____ they _____ in Woodstock? Since _____.

11. How long _____ Heather _____ in Australia? _____ she was eighteen.

12. How long _____ interested in drama? _____ she was eleven.

13. When _____ meet Harry? While _____.

14. When _____ married for the first time? _____.

15. When _____ Joanne _____? _____.

16. How long _____ married to Harry? _____.

17. How long _____ in the school in Oxford? Since _____.

18. When _____ meet Richard? _____ Christmas time in 1998.

Vocabulary

6 Suffixes and prefixes

1 Make at least one new word with each base word using the suffixes and/or prefixes. Use your dictionary to help. Sometimes you will need to change the spelling a little.

Prefix	Base word	Suffix
un-	1 possible 2 thought 3 agree	-ful
in-	4 care 5 hope 6 conscious	-less
	7 human 8 success	-able
im-	9 polite 10 help	-ness
dis-	11 understand 12 taste 13 legal	-ment
mis-	14 logical 15 stress 16 popular 17 use 18 like	-ity

1 <u>impossible   possibility   impossibility</u>
2 _____
3 _____
4 _____
5 _____
6 _____
7 _____
8 _____
9 _____
10 _____
11 _____
12 _____
13 _____
14 _____
15 _____
16 _____
17 _____
18 _____

2 Complete the sentences with the correct form of the word in brackets.

1 The school bully was very **unpopular** with all of his classmates. (popular)

2 The situation was _____ . Nobody could do anything to help. (hope)

3 Rudeness won't get you anywhere. _____ always pays! (polite)

4 Thank you very much for the information. You've been very _____ . (help)

5 His plan to become a millionaire by the age of thirty wasn't very _____. His business went bankrupt last week. (success)

6 She's very sweet and polite, _____ her brother who is very rude. (like)

7 Don't _____ me. I really want to come to your party, but I can't. (understand)

8 I don't understand. I'm really _____ about what I eat and I've been doing exercise for weeks but it's all totally _____. I'm still overweight! (care, use)

9 He caused her a lot of _____ with that _____ comment about her looking awful at the wedding. (stress, thought)

10 My husband and I usually get on really well. We only ever have _____ about where to go on holiday. (agree)

Pronunciation

7 Diphthongs

> ❗ Diphthongs are two vowel sounds which run together.
>
> | near | /nɪə/ | |
> |------|-------|---|
> | here | /hɪə/ | = /ɪ/+ /ə/   = diphthong /ɪə/ |
>
> | hair | /heə/ | |
> |-------|--------|---|
> | share | /ʃeə/ | = /e/+ /ə/   = diphthong /eə/ |

1 **T 10.2** Write the words from the box next to the correct diphthong. There are two more words for each diphthong.

where	clear	stay	shy
weigh	know	sure	now
phone	bear	high	enjoy
poor	beer	noise	aloud

1 /ɪ/ + /ə/ = /ɪə/   near   _____ _____

2 /e/ + /ə/ = /eə/   hair   _____ _____

3 /e/ + /ɪ/ = /eɪ/   pay   _____ _____

4 /ə/+ /ʊ/ = /əʊ/   go   _____ _____

5 /a/ + /ɪ/ – /aɪ/   my   _____ _____

6 /ɔ:/+ /ɪ/ = /ɔɪ/   boy   _____ _____

7 /a/ + /ʊ/ = /aʊ/   how   _____ _____

8 /ʊ/ + /ə/ = /ʊə/   tour   _____ _____

2 **T 10.3** Transcribe the words in the sentences in phonetic script. They are all diphthongs.

1 We caught the /pleɪn/ _____ to the /saʊθ/ _____ of /speɪn/ _____ .

2 The /bɔɪ/ _____ in the red /kəʊt/ _____ said that he /ɪnˈdʒɔɪd/ _____ the journey.

3 I've /nəʊn/ _____ Sally for /ˈnɪəli/ _____ /faɪv/ _____ years.

4 She's /ˈweərɪŋ/ _____ a red /rəʊz/ _____ in her /heə/ _____ .

5 Not many people /sməʊk/ _____ /paɪps/ _____ these /deɪz/ _____ .

6 He /laɪks/ _____ to /raɪd/ _____ a big black /ˈməʊtəbaɪk/ _____ .

Prepositions

8 Prepositions of time

Put the correct preposition of time into each gap.

1 Mozart wrote the tune 'Twinkle Twinkle Little Star' _____ a very young age.

2 I lived in Madrid _____ five years, _____ 1995 _____ 2001.

3 We never see our cat. He sleeps _____ the day, and he goes out _____ night.

4 I don't usually go out _____ the evening, except _____ Monday evening, when I play snooker.

5 **A** How long are you in Edinburgh for?
   B _____ six months.

6 **A** How much longer are you staying?
   B _____ the end of the month. Then I have to go home.

7 I'm just going out to get some lunch. If anyone rings, tell them I'll be back _____ half an hour.

8 Generations of my family have lived in this town _____ 1800.

9 Are you going away _____ Easter?

10 I met my husband in Wales. _____ the time I was working in a pub.

11

Indirect questions • Question tags
Idioms • Phrasal verbs – common phrasal verbs

Tell me about it!

Indirect questions

1 Yes/No questions

1 Complete the questions with the correct form of *do*, *be*, and *have*.

Quiz 1

1 <u>Is</u> the Gobi desert in Asia?

2 _____ all fish lay eggs?

3 _____ dinosaurs lay eggs?

4 _____ John F. Kennedy the youngest American president?

5 _____ there ever been a female president of the USA?

6 _____ the Olympic Games ever been held in the same city more than once?

7 _____ Japan have a president?

8 _____ John Lennon ever live in New York?

2 Now answer the questions. If you aren't sure, use these phrases.

| I don't know if … | I've no idea if … |
| I'm not sure if … | I can't remember if … |

1 <u>I've no idea if the Gobi desert is in Asia.</u>

2 _____

3 _____

4 _____

5 _____

6 _____

7 _____

8 _____

2 Wh- questions

1 Complete the questions with *what*, *when*, *where*, *who*, or *which*.

Quiz 2

1 <u>Which</u> countries have a coastline on the Mediterranean Sea?

2 _____ is measured by the Richter Scale?

3 _____ does the word 'alphabet' come from?

4 _____ was the first man in space?

5 _____ does NASA stand for?

6 _____ did Prince Rainier of Monaco marry?

7 _____ did Nelson Mandela become President of South Africa?

8 _____ Caribbean island did Bob Marley come from?

2 Now answer the questions. If you aren't sure, use these phrases.

| I don't know … | I've no idea … |
| I'm not sure … | I can't remember … |

1 <u>I'm not sure which countries have a coastline on the</u>
   <u>Mediterranean Sea.</u>

2 _____

3 _____

4 _____

5 _____

6 _____

7 _____

8 _____

3 Do you know where ...?

Complete the sentences.

1 **A** Where's the cinema?

   B I'm afraid I don't know **_where the cinema is._**

2 **A** Could you tell me _____ ?

   B I'm sorry, I haven't got a watch.

3 **A** Where have I put my keys?

   B You're always forgetting _____ !

4 **A** What are you giving your father for his birthday?

   B I haven't decided _____ yet.

5 **A** Did you post my letter?

   B I can't remember _____ or not.

6 **A** Whose coat is this?

   B I've no idea _____ .

7 **A** Are you going on the rollercoaster?

   B I'm not sure _____ .

8 **A** Do you know _____ our new teacher _____ ?

   B Yes, her name's Jenny Carter. She's over there.

9 **A** How much did Frankie's trainers cost?

   B I haven't a clue _____ .

10 **A** Where does Andrew get all his money from?

   B No idea. I'd love to know _____ his job

       _____ .

4 Newspaper headlines

Write indirect questions about the newspaper headlines.

Man wins record amount on lottery

1 he'll / away / wonder / give / I / if / any / it / of
I wonder if he'll give any of it away.

OLDEST MAN IN WORLD CELEBRATES BIRTHDAY

2 is / don't / how / he / we / know / old / exactly

_____

3 birthday / celebrate / wonder / going / I / how / he's /
his / to

_____

Bank robber escapes from prison

4 managed / how / get / nobody / out / he / knows / to

_____

5 helped / escape / wonder / who / I / to / him

_____

Actress marries husband no 7

6 know / didn't / she'd / many / I / been / so / times /
married

_____

7 if / wonder / I / this / last / be / will / time / the

_____

Shock defeat for Brazilian football team

8 know / what / like / to / the / I'd / score / was

_____

9 doesn't / headline / the / say / were / they / against /
playing / who

_____

10-year-old boy gets medical degree

10 wonder / how / I / graduated / quickly / he / so

_____

11 wonder / I / he / doctor / if / a / good / is

_____

5 Visiting a city

1 Read about Montreal. Then complete the questions below.

Montreal in Canada is the largest French-speaking city in the world next to Paris. It has a population of 2.8 million of which two thirds have French ancestry. French is the official language, but English is almost as common. There are language laws that require French writing in public places to be twice as large as English.

Montreal is situated on the Saint Lawrence Seaway and is a vital port for ships travelling to the Great Lakes and the Atlantic. It lies below Mount Royal, the ancient volcano after which the city is named. It was "discovered" in 1535 by the French explorer Jacques Cartier and is a wonderful mix of old and new – ancient stone buildings alongside modern, glass and steel.

The climate is one of extremes: summers are hot, 27°C, but winter temperatures average only -10°C and winter lasts four to five months. However, in order that you don't have to suffer such cold, they have built an underground city called 'La Ville Souterraine'. This is one of Montreal's most amazing sights with nearly 20 miles of walkways below street level. You can shop, have lunch, watch a movie, and enter a hotel without ever going outside!

The city celebrates the arts in a big way. Visitors from all over the world travel to Montreal for its many film and jazz festivals. It's also the gourmet capital of North America. Not only can you find some of the world's finest restaurants (over 5,000), but on nearly every street corner you can buy 'poutine', a delicious dish of French fries served with hot cheese and brown gravy.

All in all Montreal has much to offer. It is one of the most interesting cities in North America.

2 **T 11.1** Complete the questions about Montreal.

1 **A** Can you tell me what <u>the population of Montreal is?</u>
  B 2.8 million.

2 **A** I've no idea how many _____ .
  B Two thirds.

3 **A** Do you know what _____ ?
  B French.

4 **A** I'm not sure exactly where _____ .
  B On the Saint Lawrence Seaway, below Mount Royal.

5 **A** I haven't a clue who _____ .
  B The French explorer, Jacques Cartier, in 1535.

6 **A** I wonder what _____ like.
  B They are a wonderful mix of ancient and modern.

7 **A** Could you tell me how long _____ ?
  B About four to five months.

8 **A** Do you know why _____ ?
  B So that you can shop and keep warm in winter.

9 **A** I don't know if _____ .
  B There are lots. People come to them from all over the world.

10 **A** Have you any idea where _____ ?
  B It's sold on nearly every street corner.

Grammar revision

6 Questions with a preposition at the end

> ❶ 1 Many verbs have dependent prepositions.
> speak **to**   talk **about**   look **for**
> dance **with**   think **about**   point **at**
>
> 2 When we ask a question about the object of the sentence, the preposition usually comes at the end.
> What did you talk **about**?
> What were you looking **for**?
> Who did she dance **with**?
> What are you pointing **at**?
> What are you thinking **about**?

1 Make questions from the statements, asking about the words in *italics*.

1 **A** _Who are you looking at?_

  B I'm looking at *that man*.

2 **A** _____ ?

  B He's waiting for *his girlfriend*.

3 **A** _____ ?

  B She works for *IBM*.

4 **A** _____ ?

  B We're talking about *where to go on holiday*.

5 **A** _____ ?

  B I stayed with *some friends*.

6 **A** _____ ?

  B That bike belongs to *me*.

7 **A** _____ ?

  B The letter is from *the electricity company*.

8 **A** _____ ?

  B He died of *old age*.

9 **A** _____ ?

  B I'm worried about *the exams*.

10 **A** _____ ?

  B I'm writing to *my friend in Rome*.

11 **A** _____ ?

  B I'm staring at *the mess you've made in the kitchen*.

---

2 **T 11.2** Complete the conversations with a short question.

1 **A** Althea's getting married.

  B _Who to?_

2 **A** Come here! I want to talk to you!

  B _____ ?

3 **A** I'd like a taxi, please.

  B _____ ?

4 **A** Give me a cloth! Quick!

  B _____ ?

5 **A** I had lunch at Le Bistro yesterday.

  B _____ ?

6 **A** My parents were absolutely furious with me!

  B _____ ?

7 **A** Ssh! I'm thinking!

  B _____ ?

8 **A** Don't you think you should apologize to her?

  B _____ ?

9 **A** Pat and I had an argument, as usual.

  B _____ ?

10 **A** Eat your lunch.

  B _____ ?

    I haven't got a knife and fork!

Question tags

7 Complete the tag

Add the correct question tag.

1 Montreal's in Canada, **isn't it?**

2 You don't like onions, _____ ?

3 You're going to university, _____ ?

4 We had a lovely holiday, _____ ?

5 It's hot today, _____ ?

6 You can't use a computer, _____ ?

7 You won't forget, _____ ?

8 We don't have to go yet, _____ ?

9 You haven't met my parents, _____ ?

10 They didn't like the film, _____ ?

8 What do you say?

1 **T 11.3** Write a sentence for each situation with the verb in brackets and a question tag.

1 You're in a restaurant. Your daughter is playing with her food. You can tell she isn't happy. (like)

You don't like your food, do you?

2 You and your friend are going to a party. He doesn't like parties and looks miserable. (want)

_____ ?

3 You went to a restaurant with your brother. He had three desserts. After dinner he looks ill. (eat)

_____ ?

4 You're out shopping. Your friend sees a dress that is absolutely beautiful, so she tries it on. (is lovely)

_____ ?

5 You go to a concert. It's brilliant. What do you say to your friend as you're leaving? (was wonderful)

_____ ?

6 You're in the cinema. Your friend isn't enjoying the horror film because it's very scary. (enjoy)

_____ ?

2 **T 11.4** Ask people to do things, or ask for information, with negative question tags.

1 It's raining, and you need to go to the station. Pete has a car. Perhaps he could give you a lift.

Pete, you couldn't give me a lift to the station, could you?

2 You're broke. Maybe Sue could lend you some money.

Sue, _____ ?

3 You've lost your sunglasses. Perhaps Nuria knows where they are.

Nuria, _____ ?

4 You need a red pen. Perhaps Ravi's got one.

Ravi, _____ ?

5 You're looking for Bill. Maybe Sarah has seen him.

Sarah, _____ ?

6 You need change for a twenty-euro note. Maybe the newspaper seller could change it for you.

Excuse me, you _____ ?

3 In exercise 1, do the question tags go up or down? What about the question tags in Exercise 2?

9 Conversations

T 11.5 Write the question tags.

1 A I can't do this exercise. It's very difficult, **isn't it?**

B Don't worry. I'm here to help you.

A I'll be able to do it if I practise, **won't I?**

B Of course. It took me ages to learn.

2 A The Browns are really wealthy, _____ ?

B I know. They're always going on holiday.

A I don't know where they get their money from.

B Still, we're happy with what we've got, _____ ?

3 A You aren't going out dressed like that, _____ ?

B Why not? I can wear what I want, _____ ?

A That depends. You're wearing my jacket, _____ ?

B No, I'm not. I bought this yesterday.

4 A Callum's new car is cool, _____ ?

B Yes, it's true. But he drives much too fast, _____ ?

A You wouldn't want one like that, _____ ?

B Yes, I would. I've always wanted a car like that!

Vocabulary and pronunciation

10 A poem

1 **T 11.6** Transcribe the words in phonetic script. What animal noises are there? Read the poem aloud to yourself.

When did the world begin?

'When did the world begin and how?'
I asked /ə læm ə gəʊt ə kaʊ/.

'What's it all about and why?'
I asked /ə pɪg əz hiː went baɪ/.

'Where will the whole thing end, and when?'
I asked /ə dʌk ə guːs ə hen/.

And I copied all their answers too,
/ə kwæk ə bɑː ən ɔɪŋk ə muː/.

by Robert Clairmont

11 Onomatopoeic words

1 **T 11.7** A word that is onomatopoeic sounds like what it means. Transcribe the onomatopoeic words in these sentences.

1 The lion /rɔːd/ _____ loudly.

2 Ssh! It's a secret. I'll /ˈwɪspə/ _____ it to you.

3 She saw a dark shape in the night and she /skriːmd/ _____ .

4 He lay on the ground /ˈgrəʊnɪŋ/ _____ with pain.

5 There was a gust of wind and the door /bæŋd/ _____ shut.

6 The wine glass /smæʃt/ _____ into a thousand pieces.

7 The cat /skrætʃt/ _____ the leg of the chair.

8 He walked down the road /ˈwɪslɪŋ/ _____ a happy tune.

Phrasal verbs

12 Common phrasal verbs

1 What do these phrasal verbs mean? Use your dictionary to help you.

take up (time)	let sb down	set off
go on (= happen)	put up with	Come on!
keep on (doing sth)	come across	pick sb up
fall out with sb		

2 Complete the sentences with the correct form of the phrasal verbs from the box. Use the definition in brackets to help.

1 There's a terrible noise outside. What's _____ ? (happen)

2 I'm going to bed. I have to be at the airport by seven o'clock tomorrow morning, so I need to _____ early. (begin a journey)

3 I was tidying the attic the other day, and I _____ some old photographs of when I was a baby. (find by accident)

4 My teenage daughters are driving me crazy. I can't _____ their moods, their music, and their constant demands for money any more. (tolerate)

5 I'm going to give up tennis. I love it, but it _____ so much time, and I'm so busy at the moment. (fill or occupy)

6 Sam is broke, so he has to _____ working, even when he's ill. (continue)

7 I'll _____ you _____ at your house at 7.00 and we'll go to the night club. Make sure you're ready. (collect in a car)

8 I'm relying on you to be there tomorrow to help me. Don't _____ me _____ . (disappoint)

9 She's _____ her boyfriend again. He arrived two hours late yesterday, and she was furious. (have an argument)

10 ' _____ , Michael! We need one more goal to win this match!' (said to encourage sb to try harder)

12

Reported speech • Reporting verbs
Birth, death and marriage
Phrasal verbs – phrasal verbs with two particles

Life's great events

Reported statements and questions

1 An argument

Karen and Tom have just returned from their honeymoon in Mexico. They had a terrible time and they have just had their first big argument.

T 12.1 Read the report of the argument in Karen's diary. Then write the actual words of the argument below.

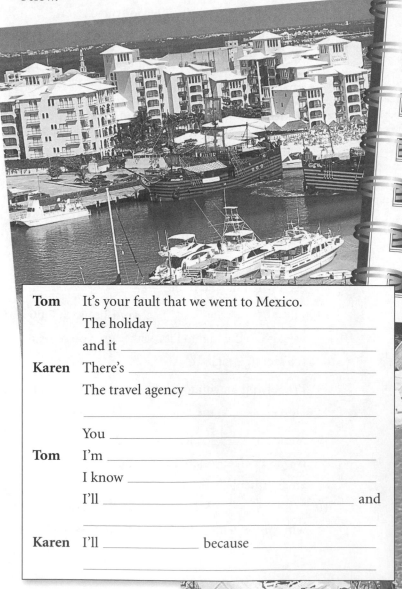

September

24 Sunday

Tom and I had our first big row last night – all about our honeymoon, of course. It was horrible! We shouted at each other!

He told me that it was my fault that we'd gone to Mexico and that the holiday had cost a fortune and had been the worst holiday he had ever had.

I said that there was nothing wrong with Mexico, it was very beautiful, but the travel agency were to blame. Their brochure had promised all kinds of things about the hotel and it had all been lies. I told him that he had no right to blame me and I started crying.

Tom said he was sorry and that he knew that it wasn't my fault really. He said that he would go to the travel agent first thing in the morning and that he would tell them about everything that had gone wrong. I said that I would go, too, because I was going to ask for our money back or another holiday.

Let's see what happens tomorrow!!

Tom	It's your fault that we went to Mexico.
	The holiday _____
	and it _____
Karen	There's _____
	The travel agency _____
	_____
	You _____
Tom	I'm _____
	I know _____
	I'll _____ and
	_____
Karen	I'll _____ because _____

2 But you said ...

T 12.2 Read the holiday brochure and complete the conversation between Tom, Karen, and the travel agent.

THE HOLIDAY OF YOUR DREAMS

honeymoons are our speciality

Location
- The hotel is twenty minutes from the airport.
- It has four acres of tropical gardens.

Facilities
- Your room will have wonderful views over the sea.
- The beautiful gardens lead directly onto the beach.
- There are two swimming pools and three tennis courts.

THE COPA DE ORA HOTEL
CANCUN, MEXICO

TA Good morning. It's Mr and Mrs Sandford, isn't it? Did you have a good time in Cancun?

T No, we did not! Where shall we begin? The transfer from the airport. Why did your brochure say that the hotel (1) **was** only twenty minutes from the airport and that it (2) _____ large tropical gardens? Not true! The drive from the airport took an hour, and where are the gardens? Your brochure said that these gardens (3) _____ directly onto the beach, but we couldn't see any tropical gardens, not even one palm tree! The next hotel had them but not ours! And you said there (4) _____ swimming pools and tennis courts – not in our hotel!

K And the rooms! You said that we (5) _____ wonderful views over the sea, but we couldn't see the sea. Only the weather was good! It was a miserable honeymoon!

3 Reporting words and thoughts

1 Report the statements.

1 'I'll miss you very much,' he said to her.
   He told her **that he'd miss her very much.**

2 'I'm going to Berlin soon.'
   She said _____ .

3 'The film will be interesting.'
   I thought _____ .

4 'I can't help you because I have too much to do.'
   She said _____ .

5 'Daniel has bought the tickets.'
   I was told _____ .

6 'I think it's a stupid idea, and it won't work.'
   She said _____
   _____ .

7 'The banks are closed on Saturdays.'
   The tour guide explained _____
   _____ .

8 'We had terrible weather on holiday.'
   He complained _____
   _____ .

9 'We've never been to Brazil,' they said to me.
   They told _____ .

2 **T 12.4** Report the questions.

1 'What are you doing?'
She asked me **what I was doing.**

2 'Do you want to go out for a walk?'
She asked me _____
_____ .

3 'Why are you crying?' he asked her.
He wondered _____
_____ .

4 'Can I borrow your car?'
He asked me _____
_____ .

5 'Where have you come from?'
The customs officer asked me _____
_____ .

6 'How long are you going to be at the gym?'
She wanted to know _____
_____ .

7 'Did you buy any milk?'
Trudi wondered _____
_____ .

8 'Will you be back early?'
She asked us _____
_____ .

9 'When do you have to go to work?'
She asked me _____
_____ .

3 **T 12.5** Write the bank manager's direct questions.

A Come and sit down, Mr Smith. Now, you want to borrow some money.
(1) **How much money do you want to borrow?**

B Five thousand pounds.

A (2) _____ ?

B Because I want to buy a car.

A I see. Could you give me some personal details?
(3) _____ ?

B I'm a graphic designer.

A And (4) _____ ?

B Thirty thousand pounds a year.

A (5) _____ ?

B Yes, I am. I've been married for six years.

A (6) _____ ?

B Yes, we've got two children.

A I see you live in a flat.
(7) _____ ?

B We've lived there for three years.

A Well, that seems fine. I don't think there'll be any problems.
(8) _____ ?

B I'd like it as soon as possible, actually.

A All right. Let's see what we can do.

4 Report the bank manager's questions.

1 First she asked Mr Smith **how much money he wanted to borrow.**

2 Then she wanted to know _____
_____ .

3 She needed to know _____
_____ .

4 He had to tell her _____
_____ .

5 Then she asked _____
_____ .

6 For some reason, she wanted to know _____
_____ .

7 She asked him _____
_____ .

8 Finally, she wondered _____
_____ .

Reported commands

4 She advised me to ...

Rewrite the sentences in reported speech using the verbs in the box.

persuade	order	ask	advise	tell
encourage	invite	beg	remind	

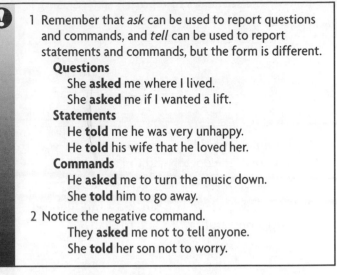

1 'If I were you, I'd go to Casualty,' he said to me.

   He advised me to go to Casualty.

2 'Could you cook dinner?' he asked Sue.

   _____

3 'Hand in your homework on Monday,' the teacher told the class.

   _____

   _____

4 'Don't forget to post the letter,' my wife said to me.

   _____

5 'Come and have dinner with us,' Marta said to Paul.

   _____

6 'You must pay a fine of two hundred pounds,' the judge said to Edward Fox.

   _____

   _____

7 'Buy the black shoes, not the brown ones,' Flora said to Emily. 'They're much, much nicer.' 'Mmm … I'm not sure. OK, I'll buy the black ones. You're right!' said Emily.

   _____

8 'You should sing professionally,' Marco said to Anthony. 'You're really good at it.'

   _____

9 'Please, please don't tell my father,' she said to me.

   _____

5 ask and tell

> **!** 1 Remember that *ask* can be used to report questions and commands, and *tell* can be used to report statements and commands, but the form is different.
>
> **Questions**
> She **asked** me where I lived.
> She **asked** me if I wanted a lift.
> **Statements**
> He **told** me he was very unhappy.
> He **told** his wife that he loved her.
> **Commands**
> He **asked** me to turn the music down.
> She **told** him to go away.
>
> 2 Notice the negative command.
> They **asked** me not to tell anyone.
> She **told** her son not to worry.

Rewrite the sentences in reported speech using *ask* or *tell*.

1 'Leave me alone!' she said to him.

   She told him to leave her alone.

2 'Please don't go,' he asked her.

   _____

3 'I'm going to bed now,' he said to Debra.

   _____

4 'How much do you earn, Dad?' asked Jeremy.

   _____

5 'Turn to page 34,' the teacher said to the class.

   _____

6 'Can you call back later, Miss Fulton?' asked the secretary.

   _____

   _____

7 'You did very well in the test,' said the teacher to the class.

   _____

   _____

8 'Don't run across the road!' the police officer told the children.

   _____

   _____

9 'Are you going to the concert?' Pam asked Roy.

   _____

10 'It's time to get up!' Harry said to his daughters.

   _____

6 Other reporting verbs

Rewrite the sentences in reported speech using the verbs in the boxes.

complain admit deny suggest boast	that …		refuse offer agree promise	to do …

1 'I think it would be a very good idea for you to go to bed,' the doctor said to Paul.

   The doctor suggested that Paul went to bed.

2 'Yes, okay. I'll lend you ten euros but I'll need it back on Saturday,' Jo said to Matt.

   _____

   _____

3 'Yes, it was me. I broke your camera,' said Harry.

   _____

   _____

4 'I didn't pull her hair,' said Timmy.

   _____

   _____

5 'I can speak eleven languages, all perfectly,' said the professor.

   _____

   _____

6 'If you finish all your homework, I'll buy you a pizza!' said Jessica's dad.

   _____

   _____

7 'Excuse me! There's a fly in my salad,' said Patrick.

   _____

   _____

8 'I'm sorry. I can't marry you because I don't love you,' Sarah said to Adrian.

   _____

   _____

9 'I'll cook supper if you like,' Amanda said to Duncan.

   _____

   _____

7 *speak* and *talk*

> **!** 1 In British English, we usually use the preposition *to* with the verbs *speak* and *talk*. American English prefers *with*.
>   Can I speak **to** you for a minute?
>   Come and talk **to** me when you're free.
> 2 *Talk* suggests that two or more people are having a conversation. It is more common than *speak*.
>   We stayed up all night **talking**.
> 3 *Speak* suggests something serious or more formal.
>   I have a complaint. I'd like to **speak** to the manager.
>   The doctor **spoke** to them about the dangers of smoking.
>   Professor Smith is going to **speak** at the conference.
> 4 *Talk* usually suggests the idea of a conversation. *Speak* can refer just to the use of words.
>   I've lost my voice. I can't **speak**.

Complete the conversation with the correct form of the verbs in the box. Careful! Some verbs are used more than once.

say   tell   explain   speak   talk   reply   ask

WAS WALKING in town the other day when I met old Mr Brown, so we stopped and (1) **talked** for a while. He (2) _____ me that his wife, Jenny, had been taken into hospital. I (3) _____ him how Jenny was, and he (4) _____ that she was getting better. I (5) _____ Mr Brown to give Jenny my regards. He wondered why I hadn't been to the tennis club recently, so I (6) _____ that I'd been very busy and just hadn't had time.

'There's something you must (7) _____ me,' Mr Brown suddenly said. 'How many languages does your son (8) _____ ?'

'Four,' I (9) _____ .'Why (10) _____ you _____ ?'

'Well, I know your son has some very funny stories to (11) _____ about his trips abroad and his language learning. We're having a meeting of the Travellers' Club next week, and I'd like him to come along and (12) _____ to us.'

I (13) _____ that I would (14) _____ to my son about it, and I promised to get back in touch with him.

Then we (15) _____ goodbye and went our separate ways.

Vocabulary

8 Birth, death, and marriage

1 Complete the sentences with the words in the box.

birth	birthday	born

1 Where were you **born**?

2 When is your _____?

3 I was _____ in Africa.

4 She gave _____ to a beautiful healthy boy.

5 (On an official form) PLACE OF _____

6 Congratulations on the _____ of little Albert.

7 What are you doing for your _____ this year?

2 Complete the sentences with the words in the box.

dying	dead	died	death	die

1 Shakespeare **died** in 1616.

2 Her father's _____ came as a great shock. He was only 45.

3 Those flowers have _____. Throw them away.

4 Every winter thousands of birds _____ in the cold weather.

5 **A** Is old Bertie Harrison still alive?

   B I'm sure he's _____. Didn't he _____ a few years ago?

6 Our poor old cat is _____. We've had her for fifteen years. She just sleeps all day long.

7 He was stabbed to _____ by a maniac in a dark alley.

8 She screamed when she saw the _____ body lying across the carpet.

9 I'm sorry to hear about your dog. When did it _____? What did it _____ of?

!
1 The verb *marry* is used without a preposition.
   My sister **married** a plumber.

2 *Get married* refers to the change of state between being single and being married.
   We **got married** in 1980.

3 *Married* refers to the state.
   Is your brother **married**?

4 *Get married* and *be married* can both be used with the preposition *to*.
   She **got married** to Gary last weekend.
   My sister is **married** to a really nice guy.

5 *Divorce* is used in a similar way to *marry*.
   Helen wants to **divorce** Keith.
   Jane and Harry **got divorced** last year.
   My brother is **divorced**.

3 Complete the sentences with the words in the box.

get married	marry	got married
married	been married	wedding

1 **A** Are you **married**?

   B No, I'm single. But I'd like to some day.

2 **A** Whatever happened to Ann?

   B She met a German boy one week and _____ him the next.

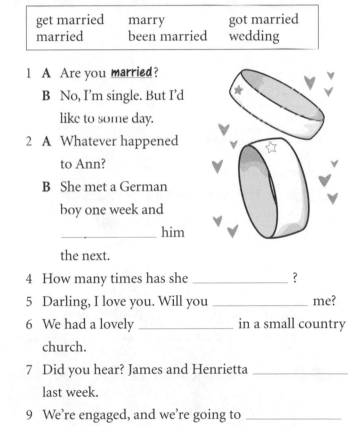

4 How many times has she _____?

5 Darling, I love you. Will you _____ me?

6 We had a lovely _____ in a small country church.

7 Did you hear? James and Henrietta _____ last week.

9 We're engaged, and we're going to _____ next autumn.

Pronunciation

9 Word stress

T 12.6 All these words appear in Unit 12 of the Student's Book. Put them in the correct columns.

honeymoon	forever	actually
cancelled	announcement	terrible
marriage	complained	opposite
counsellor	colleague	reception
invite	engaged	bouquet
reminded	accused	funeral

A	B	C	D
● ● ●	● ●	● ● ●	● ●

10 *had* or *would*?

1 **T 12.7** Read the sentences. Does *'d* mean *had* or *would*?

1 We'd love to meet your mother. **would**

2 They asked if we'd give them a lift. _____

3 They asked if we'd given her the present yet. _____

4 We asked when they'd met each other. _____

5 We asked when they'd see each other again. _____

6 After my accident, the doctor said I'd never ski again. _____

2 **T 12.8** Transcribe these sentences. Does *'d* mean *had* or *would*?

1 /ʃi: sed ðət ʃi:d si:n hɪm/ _____

2 /ʃi: sed ðət ʃi:d si: hɪm su:n/ _____

3 /hi təʊld hə hi:d lʌvd hə fər ə lɒŋ taɪm/ _____

4 /hi təʊld hə hi:d lʌv hə fərevə/ _____

Phrasal verbs

11 Phrasal verbs with two particles

Complete the sentences with a phrasal verb from the box. Careful! Some are used more than once.

back on	away from	out of
forward to	on with	down on
up with		

1 We've run **out of** sugar. Could you buy some more?

2 We must try to cut _____ the amount of money we spend. We're always broke.

3 Please don't let me disturb you. Carry _____ your work.

4 Keep _____ me! I've got a terrible cold, and I don't want you to catch it.

5 How do you get _____ your parents? OK?

6 I don't know how you put _____ such noisy brothers. It would drive me crazy.

7 When I look _____ my childhood, I realize how unhappy I was.

8 I'm really looking _____ our holidays next week. I'm so excited!

9 Children grow _____ their clothes so quickly. It costs a fortune!

Revision

Tenses

1 Naming the tenses

Match the sentences in **A** with the tenses in **B**.

A

1 ☑ *d* Do elephants eat meat?
2 ☐ People haven't been using the Internet for thirty years.
3 ☐ I've had this book for a week.
4 ☐ Portuguese is spoken in Brazil.
5 ☐ The Egyptians built the Pyramids.
6 ☐ What were you doing an hour ago?
7 ☐ When was the film *Titanic* made?
8 ☐ If you are looking at the Vatican, which city are you standing in?

B

a Past Simple
b Present Continuous
c Present Simple passive
d Present Simple
e Past Continuous
f Past Simple passive
g Present Perfect simple
h Present Perfect continuous

2 Questions and negatives

Put the words in the correct order to make a question or a negative.

1 move. The doesn't sun
The sun doesn't move.

2 in film? Madonna been a Has
_____

3 French doing not a exercise. I'm
_____

4 wasn't president 1984. He in
_____

5 haven't any got children. They
_____

6 after Where going you the are lesson?
_____

7 does mean? What 'perform'
_____

8 you a lunch? Did for have sandwich
_____

9 learning you English? Do enjoy
_____

Write true short answers for 8 and 9.
_____
_____

Present tenses

1 Present Simple or Present Continuous?

Put the verbs in brackets into the correct form, Present Simple or Present Continuous.

1 She **plays** (play) golf with her husband.
2 I _____ (not eat) lunch today.
3 Some birds _____ (fly) to warm countries in the winter.
4 We never _____ (go) on holiday at Christmas.
5 Why _____ she _____ (do) the washing-up? Is it her turn?
6 Our cousins _____ (not visit) us very often.
7 _____ you _____ (fix) computers?
8 _____ (be) they always late for meetings?
9 Wear your boots. It _____ (snow).
10 We _____ (have) dinner together next Monday.
11 No, I _____ (not live) in Rome, I _____ (live) in Milan.
12 He _____ (work) for an international company so he _____ (travel) a lot in his job.
13 We _____ (study) very hard at the moment.
14 Next week she _____ (go) to Madrid on business.

2 State verbs

Read the pairs of sentences. Tick the correct ones.

1 a Who is this coat belonging to?
   b Who does this coat belong to? ✓
2 a They have ten grandchildren.
   b They are having ten grandchildren.
3 a Do you enjoy the film?
   b Are you enjoying the film?
4 a I'm going to the dentist's before work, so I'll be late.
   b I go to the dentist's before work, so I'll be late.
5 a I always take the bus to work.
   b I'm always taking the bus to work.
6 a This fish smells bad.
   b This fish is smelling bad.
7 a They are having a baby in June.
   b They have a baby in June.

3 Present passive

Complete the passive sentences.

1 A lot of people in Canada play ice hockey.
   A lot of ice hockey **is played** in Canada.
2 They keep the results on a computer.
   The results _____ on a computer.
3 Her mother is helping her to do her homework.
   She _____ by her mother.
4 The invitation says 'arrive at 12.30'.
   Guests _____ to arrive at 12.30.
5 They pay me on the first day of the month.
   I _____ on the first day of the month.
6 Their grandparents are taking them holiday.
   They _____ on holiday by their grandparents.
7 They're building 400 new houses there.
   400 new houses _____ there.
8 They throw unsold sandwiches away each day.
   Unsold sandwiches _____ away each day.

Past tenses

1 Past Simple or Past Continuous?

Complete the conversations with the Past Simple or the Past Continuous form of the verbs in brackets.

1 A Sorry I **didn't meet** (not meet) you at the railway station – I **was waiting** (wait) at the bus station.
   B That's OK. I _____ (wait) for fifteen minutes then I _____ (take) a taxi.

2 A She _____ (not look) very happy this morning.
   B She _____ (not be)! Someone _____ (phone) while she _____ (sleep).
3 A _____ you _____ (watch) the football last night?
   B Yes, I _____ (see) it while I _____ (do) the ironing.
4 A _____ you _____ (look) for me earlier?
   B Yes, I _____ (want) to ask you something.
5 A I _____ (start) skiing when I _____ (live) in Austria last year.
   B I _____ (not know) you'd lived there.

2 Past Simple or Past Perfect?

Complete the sentences with the Past Simple or the Past Perfect forms of the verbs in brackets.

1 He **bought** (buy) her a ring after he **had known** (know) her for a week.
2 I _____ (not ring) him because I _____ (forgot) to take his number with me.
3 He _____ (not pass) his driving test when he _____ (drive) from San Francisco to LA!
4 When I _____ (get) home, I _____ (remember) that I _____ (leave) the baby in the shop.
5 He _____ (not know) how the cat _____ (walk) 100 kilometres to its old home.
6 She only _____ (hear) about the interview three months after she _____ (apply) for the job.
7 When he first _____ (go) to Moscow he _____ (never travel) abroad before.
8 They _____ (not enjoy) the film because they _____ (see) it before.
9 That's a surprise! I _____ (not know) you two _____ (meet) already.
10 They _____ (be) married for five years when they _____ (have) their first child.

3 A short story

Complete the story with the Past Simple, Past Continuous or Past Perfect form of the verb in brackets.

They **had lived** (live) in the village for over three years but they (1) _____ (never meet) the woman who (2) _____ (own) the house on the corner. A large tree (3) _____ (stand) outside the front door and the curtains (4) _____ (be) always drawn. Nobody (5) _____ (know) much about her – even the postman, who (6) _____ (seem) to know everything about everyone! One day, though, when they (7) _____ (walk) past her house, they (8) _____ (notice) that the front door (9) _____ (be) open and so they (10) _____ (decide) to see if everything (11) _____ (be) OK. As they (12) _____ (walk) up the path, they (13) _____ (can) hear a noise. A woman (14) _____ (cry). They (15) _____ (go) inside and (16) _____ (find) the woman. She (17) _____ (lie) in the hallway. She (18) _____ (fall) ill and (19) _____ (manage) to open the door. She (20) _____ (be) very pleased to see them!

4 Past passive

Complete the sentences with the Past Simple passive form of the verb in brackets.

1 The Picasso museum in Barcelona **was opened** in 1988.
2 *Guernica* _____ (paint) to record the bombing of a Basque village.
3 Hemingway _____ (send) to France during the First World War.
4 *The Great Gatsby* and *Tender is the Night* _____ (write) by Scott Fitzgerald.
5 He _____ (not bring) up in Paris.
6 A lot of young artist and writers _____ (help) by Gertrude Stein.

Modal verbs 1

1 Questions and negatives

Read the sentences. Write (1) the negative, (2) the question and (3) the third person singular.

1 I can use his car.
   1 **I can't use his car.**
   2 _____
   3 She/He _____

2 I should write to them.
   1 _____
   2 _____
   3 She/He _____

4 I must phone them.
   1 _____
   2 _____
   3 She/He _____

2 Signs

Read the signs. Match them with the meanings.

1 | No parking at any time | _c_
2 | DO NOT LEAVE BAGS UNATTENDED | ___
3 | *Please take all your belongings with you* | ___
4 | NO VISITORS BEYOND THIS POINT | ___
5 | Please help yourself to tea or coffee | ___
6 | Hotel guests are invited to join the manager for pre-dinner drinks | ___

a You can have a drink.
b You have to keep your luggage with you.
c ~~You must put your car in another place.~~
d You mustn't go any further.
e You don't have to go to the party.
f You shouldn't leave anything behind.

Future forms

1 Correcting mistakes

In each of these sentences there is a mistake with a future form. Find it and correct it.

1 I going to see her tomorrow.

   I'm going to see her tomorrow.

2 Greg will helping you move the computer.

   _____

3 Don't ask Al, he isn't help you.

   _____

4 Kate catch the train at 3.30 this afternoon.

   _____

5 They don't visit us next summer.

   _____

6 Are you go meet them at the airport?

   _____

2 Choosing the correct form

Choose the correct answers.

1 What are you doing this evening?
   a I'll go to the cinema.
   b I'm going to the cinema. ✓

2 Are you going to the bank?
   a Yes, I'll go there to talk to the manager.
   b Yes, I'm going there to talk to the manager.

3 Have you got plans for the weekend?
   a I'm playing golf with Chris.
   b I'll play golf with Chris.

4 This lesson is so boring.
   a Don't worry. It's finished soon.
   b Don't worry, it'll finish soon.

5 Where are you going for Christmas?
   a I'm not sure – I think I'll stay here.
   b I'm not sure – I'm staying here.

6 I've booked the tickets but I can't collect them.
   a It's OK, I'm going into town so I'll collect them.
   b It's OK, I'm going into town so I am collecting them.

7 Have you seen Tom yet?
   a No, he's arriving on the 6 o'clock train.
   b No, he'll arrive on the 6 o'clock train.

8 Look at those dark clouds!
   a Oh dear, it'll rain.
   b Oh dear, it's going to rain.

3 A conversation

Read the conversation. Underline the correct future forms.

A _I'm going_ / _'ll go_ to town. Do you want anything?

B _Are you going_ / _Will you go_ to the post office? I need forty stamps.

A Yes, I am. I _will apply_ / _am applying_ for a new driving licence so I'll get you the stamps at the same time.

B Thanks.

A Why do you need forty stamps? You always send emails.

B Well I _'m having_ / _'ll have a party_, so I want to send invitations to everybody.

A If you want me to, I _'m buying_ / _'ll buy_ the invitations too.

B Thanks, but I _'m getting_ / _'ll get_ them printed at work. It's already arranged.

A OK. I _'ll see_ / _'m seeing_ you later! Bye.

Questions with _like_

Choosing the correct question

Choose the correct questions.

1 A a What does he look like? ✓
     b What's he like?
   B He's tall, dark and handsome.

2 A a What would you like to do?
     b What do you like doing?
   B I'd like to go out for lunch.

3 A a What are Hemingway's books like?
     b Do you like Hemingway's books?
   B Yes, I do.

4 A a What's she like?
     b What does she like doing?
   B She's quiet but friendly.

5 A a What do you like doing at the weekends?
     b What was your weekend like?
   B It was a bit boring. I had to stay at home because I was ill.

6 A a What kind of food do you like?
     b What kind of food would you like?
   B Let's go for a Chinese meal.

Verb patterns

-ing or infinitive?

Complete the sentences with the correct form of the verb in brackets.

1 The garage promised **to have** the car ready at 4.30.
2 He asked the student in the next room _____ (turn) her TV down.
3 We all enjoy _____ (spend) money.
4 My boss asked me _____ (train) the new office assistant.
5 We decided _____ (wait) for another hour.
6 She starts _____ (work) here next week.
7 I'd love _____ (go) to Spain with you.
8 I remember _____ (speak) to him at the party.
9 I can't stand _____ (wait)!
10 He said he hoped _____ (arrive) at 10.00.

Present Perfect

1 Form and short answers

Complete the conversation with the Present Perfect form of the verbs in brackets and short answers.

A How long **have you been** (be) in Paris?
B For two weeks.
A _____ you _____ (start) your new job?
B No, I **haven't**. I start next week.
A _____ you _____ (find) somewhere to live?
B No, I _____. I _____ (see) a few apartments but I haven't found the right one yet.
A _____ you _____ (visit) any of the museums and galleries?
B Yes, I _____. I _____ (go) to the Louvre and the Musée D'Orsay but I _____ (not go) to the Musée Rodin yet.
A And what about your French lessons? _____ your course _____ (start) yet?
B Oh yes, it _____. It's a really nice class.
A Well, good luck. I hope the job goes well and that you find a flat soon.

2 Present Perfect or Past Simple?

Complete the sentences with the correct form of the verb in brackets.

1 Ana **hasn't been** (not go) on holiday yet this summer.
2 Daisy and Jane _____ (not receive) their exam results last week.
3 I _____ (learn) to swim when I was a child.
4 I _____ (work) in Tokyo in 2001.
5 Leon _____ (go) to school in Dublin until he was twelve.
6 Ute _____ (live) in this house since she was a baby.
7 We _____ (be) married since last autumn.
8 _____ you ever _____ (win) anything in a competition?
9 She _____ (not speak) to him since their divorce.
10 Jan _____ (not go) abroad since a business trip in 1998.

3 Present Perfect active and passive

Complete the news with verbs from the box in the Present Perfect, active or passive.

sink put leave cause award ~~arrive~~ arrest

Here are the news headlines.

The Spanish Prime Minister (1) **has arrived** in London for two days of talks with the British government.

An oil tanker (2) _____ off the north coast of France.

High winds and heavy rain (3) _____ serious damage to coastal areas in the south. Four hundred people (4) _____ their homes and (5) _____ in emergency accommodation.

Footballer Keith Waites (6) _____ after a nightclub fight in Barcelona.

And finally – the prize for best film (7) _____ to The Hours.

Conditionals

1 First conditional

There is one mistake in each sentence. Find it and correct it.

1 Where do you live if you can't find a flat?

Where will you live if you can't find a flat?

2 If you will run, you'll catch the train.

_____

_____

3 I won't ring you, unless I'll be late.

_____

_____

4 If it be sunny, we'll go to the beach.

_____

_____

5 I won't go to the football match if Beckham can't playing.

_____

_____

6 She will be very unhappy if he won't ring her.

_____

_____

2 Second conditional

Complete the second conditional sentences so they are true for you.

1 If a friend gave me a horrible present, I **'d just smile and say thank you.**

2 I'd be very surprised if _____

3 My best friend would be very angry if _____

_____

4 If I saw a bank robbery, I _____

_____

5 If I found an expensive watch, I _____

_____

6 If I won €2 million, I _____

_____

7 If I could go anywhere in the world, I _____

_____

8 I would never go to an English class again if _____

_____

3 Zero, first or second conditional?

1 Complete the sentences with the correct form of the verb in brackets.

1 If you cook, I **'ll wash up** (wash up).

2 If you go to the cinema before 6 p.m., the seats _____ (be) cheaper.

3 I'd be very angry if you _____ (forget) my birthday.

4 If I see her, I _____ (tell) her.

5 If I saw a ghost, I _____ (take) a photograph of it.

6 I _____ (not run) into a house if it were on fire.

7 Use the stairs if there _____ (be) a fire.

8 We _____ (be) late if we don't go now.

9 If I _____ (have) his address, I'd write him a letter.

Modal verbs 2

Possibility/probability

Match the sentences in **A** and **B**.

A	
1	[h] They must be in love.
2	☐ She couldn't have taken the car.
3	☐ They can't have paid the bill.
4	☐ I didn't receive the flowers.
5	☐ This letter has been returned.
6	☐ I might not be able to see you on Wednesday.
7	☐ She often works late on a Monday.
8	☐ He can't be in New York.
9	☐ Lend you my car?

B

a The shop could have sent them to the wrong address.

b They must have moved house.

c Her keys are here.

d I saw him ten minutes ago.

e You must be joking!

f She might still be at the office.

g Their phone's been cut off.

h They are always together.

i I might have to baby sit.

Present Perfect Simple or Continuous?

1 Choosing the correct form

Underline the correct verb in each sentence.

1 I wish they'd arrive – I *'ve been waiting* / *'ve waited* for more than hour.
2 Look at all that water! It *'s been raining* / *'s rained* very hard.
3 I *'ve been cleaning* / *'ve cleaned* the car this week.
4 Wow! You *'ve cooked* / *'ve been cooking* dinner! Let's eat now.
5 He *'s been buying* / *'s bought* some flowers for her birthday and now he's looking for a card.
6 I *'ve been cleaning* / *'ve cleaned* all day. I *'ve been doing* / *'ve done* the bedrooms and now I'm doing the bathroom.
7 She *has been sleeping* / *has slept* downstairs because she has broken her leg.
8 We *have looked* / *have been looking* for a hotel for two hours.

2 Sentence completion

Complete the sentences with suitable words.

1 Where have you **been** ? You're over half an hour late.
2 He's been _____ for a flat for months but he still _____ found one.
3 Tom's been _____ in London for the last few months, but he hasn't _____ whether to stay there.
4 How long have you been _____ here? Do you like your job?
5 What have you _____? There is glass on the floor!
6 'Have you _____ James?' 'No, I think he's _____ out.'
7 I've been _____ at this computer all morning and I have only _____ one letter.
8 She's been _____ to make a phone call for half an hour but she still hasn't _____ through.
9 I haven't _____ reading the book yet. In fact, I've only _____ the first three chapters.
10 Have you _____ the news? United have _____ the match.

Indirect questions

1 An interview

Think of a famous person. You are going to interview them. Write indirect questions.
Use *I'd like to know … I wonder … Could you tell me …?*

1 when he/she was born
   I'd like to know when you were born.
2 where he/she went to school
   _____
3 when he/she started …. (singing/acting/playing football, etc.)
   _____
4 if he/she is married
   _____
5 if he/she has any children
   _____
6 if he/she enjoys being famous
   _____
7 what plans he/she has
   _____
8 *your question*
   _____

2 Correcting mistakes

In each of the following sentences there is a mistake. Find it and correct it.

1 I'm sorry but I don't know what time is it.
   I'm sorry but I don't know what time it is.
2 I've no idea where does he live.
   _____
3 Do you happen to know when did he arrive?
   _____
4 I wonder where has he been all day.
   _____
5 Oh dear! I've completely forgotten what was I doing.
   _____
6 That's strange! I wonder where has he put it.
   _____
7 I haven't a clue what does he think.
   _____
8 Could you let me know when are you ready?
   _____

Question tags

Complete the questions with the correct question tag.

1 She can swim, **can't she** ?
2 The food isn't very good, _____ ?
3 You haven't seen my glasses, _____ ?
4 He's coming to the party, _____ ?
5 I didn't send you a birthday card, _____ ?
6 You've got your keys, _____ ?
7 That was a stupid thing to do, _____ ?
8 You won't be late, _____ ?
9 He lives near you, _____ ?
10 He hadn't heard the news, _____ ?

Reported speech

1 Reported statements and questions

Report the sentences.

1 'I'm going to the station.'
   He said he **was going to the station** .
2 'We've got some champagne in the fridge.'
   She said they _____ .
3 'I saw him yesterday.'
   He said he _____ .
4 'I don't know the answer.'
   He told me he _____ .
5 'We lived in London a long time ago.'
   She said they _____ .
6 'I haven't known him long.'
   She said she _____ .
7 'What is your girlfriend's name?'
   I asked him _____ .
8 'Which school did you go to?'
   I asked her _____ .
9 'Have you seen the news today?'
   I asked him _____ that day.
10 Where does your friend work?'
   I asked her _____ .
11 'How long are you staying?'
   She asked them _____ .
12 'What time does it begin?'
   I asked him _____ .

2 Reporting verbs

Complete the sentences. Use the correct form of the verb in the box.

advise ask invite order refuse remind tell

1 'Please come to our wedding.'
   They **invited** me to their wedding.
2 'You should save some money.'
   The bank manager _____ me to save some money.
3 'No, I'm sorry but I won't work late this evening.'
   I _____ to stay late at the office on Friday evening.
4 'Get out of your car.'
   The police officer _____ me to get out of my car.
5 'Can you tell me what the time is?'
   He _____ me what the time was.
6 'Don't forget to put the cat out.'
   She _____ me to put the cat out.
7 'Put the letters on the table, please.'
   She _____ him to put the letters on the table.

Key

1 1 I like skiing.
I don't like snowboarding.
Do you like skiing?
My father likes skiing.
My mother doesn't like skiing.
Does your father like skiing?
2 I'm studying English.
I'm not studying Spanish.
Are you studying English?
My father's studying English.
My mother isn't studying English.
Is your father studying English?
3 I saw the Empire State Building.
I didn't see the Statue of Liberty.
Did you see the Empire State Building?
My father saw the Empire State Building.
My mother didn't see the Empire State Building.
Did your father see the Empire State Building?
4 I've met Muhammad Ali.
I haven't met Pelé.
Have you met Muhammad Ali?
My father's met Muhammad Ali.
My mother hasn't met Muhammad Ali.
Has your father met Muhammad Ali?

2 3 A 4 F 5 F 6 A 7 F 8 F 9 A
10 A 11 A 12 F

3 2 She's got two brothers and she doesn't get on with either of them.
3 He has no brothers and sisters – he's an only child.
4 We weren't happy with the hotel so we didn't stay there for long.
5 He didn't go to the party because he had a cold.
6 They're getting married when they've saved enough money.
7 John isn't sure where Jill is.
8 She's parking the car. It's always difficult in our street.
9 I don't want them to know who I am.
10 Don't you understand what I'm saying?

4 1 1 1 've 2 isn't 3 's 4 don't 5 'm
6 was 7 don't 8 did 9 didn't
10 have 11 haven't 12 does
2 1 Why is Phil ringing the Computer Helpline?
Because he's got a problem with his computer.
2 Which company does Phil work for?
He doesn't work for a company.
He's self-employed.
3 What was he doing when his computer stopped?
He was working away happily.
4 Why can't Phil remember the message?
Because he didn't understand it.
5 Has he switched his computer off?
No, he hasn't.

5 2 What are you wearing at the moment?
3 Do you play any sports at the weekend?
4 What time did you get up this morning?
5 Have you ever met a famous person?
6 Do you look like your mother?
7 Where did you go on holiday when you were a child?

6 Student's own answers
2 What languages does he speak?
3 What did you get?
4 How much did they pay?
5 How many kittens did she have?
6 What film is she going to see?
7 What's he going to buy?/Where's he going?
8 Where did you go?
9 What do you do?/Why is it interesting?
10 Who's she talking to?

7 1 3 hasn't 4 am 5 don't 6 didn't
7 have 8 do 9 did 10 isn't
2 **Sample answers**
2 Yes, I am. I'm going skiing.
3 No, we didn't. It rained every day!
4 No, I haven't – but I'd like to go.
5 Yes, I do. I have to travel in my job.
6 No, she doesn't. I always go with my family.

8 3 've got/have 4 's got/has 5 'll have
6 haven't got/don't have 7 's had
8 're having 9 have 10 Did you have
11 Have you got/Do you have 12 does she usually have

9 1

Adjective	Noun
musical	music
scientific	science
happy	happiness
greedy	greed
dangerous	danger
wonderful	wonder

Noun	Verb
achievement	achieve
competition	compete
discussion	discuss
organization	organize
appearance	appear
exploration	explore

2 1 musical 2 invite 3 wonder
4 scientific 5 dangerous 6 discussion
7 greedy 8 organization
9 competition 10 explore

10 2 c 3 g 4 i 5 a 6 j 7 b 8 f 9 d 10 h

11 2 e 3 g 4 d 5 c 6 b 7 i 8 k 9 o
10 a 11 l 12 n 13 j 14 m 15 h

12

A	B	C
president	breakfast	afford
happiness	business	believe

D	E
computer	penicillin
important	politician

13 2 the birds to build a nest
3 the moon is not quite round
4 lights the stars
5 the rainbow in the sky

14 1 with 2 in 3 about 4 to 5 to
6 about 7 on 8 of 9 for 10 about
11 for 12 with

1 Maria Hernandez 2, 5, 7
Vichai 1, 3, 6
Uma and Sanjit Singh 8, 4, 9

2 2 sell 3 doesn't close/is open 4 don't
visit 5 has 6 takes 7 finishes
8 doesn't provide 9 graduate, want
10 have/eat 11 earn/make 12 hate

3 1 What does the corner shop sell?
2 What time does it open?
3 Why don't Uma and Sanjit go to the movies any more?
4 Where does Maria's father work?
5 Where does she live?
6 How many students are in each class at her school?
7 What languages do her teachers speak?
8 How does she usually go to school?
9 What does she want to do when she finishes school?
10 Who does Vichai live with??
11 What does he enjoy playing?
12 Does he like living in Bangkok?

4 2 An atheist doesn't believe in God.
3 In Britain, police officers don't carry guns.
4 Selfish people don't think of other people.
5 Real Madrid players don't wear red.
6 I'm unemployed. I haven't got/don't have a job.
7 My father's bald. He hasn't got any hair.
9 They're penniless. They haven't got any money.
10 Kangaroos don't live in Mexico.

5

/s/	/z/	/ɪz/
products	boys	closes
minutes	lives	messages
graduates	hours	sandwiches
wants	earns	
hates	loves	
cooks	lessons	
	things	

6 Sample answers
Rita – At work
Rita is a basketball coach. Every weekday she works with the players. They train hard, and practise moves. She wears a tracksuit and trainers.
Now
At the moment she isn't working; she's in her kitchen. She's wearing a blouse and skirt. She's giving her children a meal.
Graeme and Sally – At work
Graeme and Sally are organic farmers. They get up very early and work in the fields most days. They grow vegetables, and raise chickens on their farm. They wear boots and old clothes.
Now
At the moment they aren't working.

They're on holiday in the Caribbean. They're having a cool drink on the beach. They're wearing shorts, shirts and sunglasses.

7 1 1 I think you should go to the dentist.
2 ✓
3 Why are you leaving so early? Aren't you enjoying the party?
4 Nobody ever laughs at my husband's jokes. It's so embarrassing.
5 ✓ 6 ✓
7 I don't see how I can help you.
8 ✓
9 He never knows the answer.

2 **Conversation 1**
1 's that man doing 2 's waiting
3 don't open 4 Do you think
5 's taking 6 's walking
Conversation 2
7 are you doing 8 'm packing 9 'm leaving 10 don't understand 11 are you going 12 don't know 13 know
14 is meeting

3 1 I'm thinking, I think
2 Do you see, are you seeing
3 have, 're having

8 2 ✓
3 I never have anything to eat in the morning.
4 ✓
5 I sometimes go abroad on business.
6 I never have enough money.
7 ✓
8 Our teacher always gives us too much homework.
9 Sonja is always late for class.

9 2 Nokia phones are produced in Finland.
3 Service is included in the bill.
4 Our kitchen is being redecorated at the moment.
5 Champagne is made in France.
6 Our company is being taken over by another company.
7 About 1,000 people are employed by the company.
8 All our vegetables are grown on the farm.
9 That block of flats is being pulled down because it is unsafe.
10 Our newspapers are delivered before breakfast.

10 1 arrive 2 are checked 3 keep 4 are taken 5 is checked 6 are x-rayed 7 are given 8 is searched 9 wait 10 is called 11 are told 12 board 13 are shown

11
	Adjective	Opposite (adj+prefix)	Opposite (dif. word)
1	polite	impolite	rude
2	expensive	inexpensive	cheap
3	interesting	uninteresting	boring
4	correct	incorrect	wrong
5	attractive	unattractive	ugly
6	fashionable	unfashionable	out of date
7	intelligent	unintelligent	stupid
8	usual	unusual	strange/rare
9	kind	unkind	cruel
10	formal	informal	casual
11	modest	immodest	arrogant

12 2 2 looking for 3 Look out
4 look forward/'m looking forward
5 look it up 6 look after
3 1 in 2 away 3 on 4 off 5 up to
6 up 7 up/in, on 8 off 9 off 10 up

UNIT 3

1 1 **Past Simple**
[2] ran up [8] killed [5] arrived
[6] put up [2] called [3] rang
[6] rescued [8] ran him over
[2] couldn't get down [7] invited them in for tea [4] tried to tempt him down
Past Continuous
[4] was waiting [1] was watering the plants [8] were leaving [1] was playing
[7] were having tea
2 2 was playing 3 ran up 4 called
5 couldn't get down 6 rang 7 was waiting 8 tried to tempt him down
9 arrived 10 put up 11 rescued
12 invited them in for tea 13 were having tea 14 were leaving 15 ran him over 16 killed

2 2 Mrs Taylor wasn't cutting the grass, she was watering the plants.
3 Billy wasn't sleeping in the garden, he was playing.
4 Billy didn't jump over the wall, he ran up a tree.
5 Mrs Taylor didn't ring the police, she rang the Fire Brigade.
6 The Fire Brigade didn't use a rope, they used a ladder.

3 2 was reading, went, heard
3 stood, walked, closed
4 walked, was carrying
5 Didn't you meet, were living
6 saw, were sitting
7 walked, handed
8 was listening, was doing
9 didn't they visit, were staying
10 were you writing, crashed

4 2 left 3 was raining 4 landed 5 was shining 6 was blowing 7 took 8 was checking in 9 tapped 10 could not
11 was staying 12 went 13 saw 14 was getting 15 returned 16 spent 17 felt
18 ended

5 2 He pulled the young man out of the van and took him straight to hospital.
3 He was watching TV when he heard the good news.
4 He gave his wife a big kiss and took his whole family out for an expensive meal.
5 People were standing in queues chatting to each other when the robbers burst in.
6 He suffered a heart attack and was taken to hospital.

6 2 while 3 for 4 While 5 for
6 During 7 for 8 while 9 during
10 during 11 for 12 while 13 during

7
Infinitive	Past Simple	Past participle
fall	fell	fallen
find	found	found
sell	sold	sold
feel	felt	felt
drive	drove	driven
fly	flew	flown
leave	left	left
travel	travelled	travelled
lie	lied	lied
win	won	won
spend	spent	spent

8 2 had been 3 had lived 4 was
5 hadn't managed 6 had taken 7 had been 8 went 9 made 10 felt 11 was
12 had been 13 decided

9 2 Jane was furious because she had overslept and (had) missed the bus.
3 He hadn't studied enough and had failed his exams.
4 Before his accident, Peter had been the best player in the team.
5 I had never flown before.
6 He had done the same job for ten years.
7 I was sure I had seen him somewhere before.
8 I hadn't had anything to eat all day.

10 3 would 4 would 5 had 6 had
7 would 8 had 9 had 10 would

11 **Helen Keller**
2 didn't know 3 found 4 were told
5 came 6 taught 7 had 8 was offered
9 toured 10 was made
Charles Blondin
2 was taught 3 became 4 was put
5 walked 6 watched 7 were carried
8 fell 9 wasn't killed 10 died
Amy Johnson
2 was taught 3 was introduced 4 held
5 tried 6 didn't succeed 7 returned
8 were married 9 was written
10 disappeared

12 3 The lights were left on.
4 I was told about it yesterday.
5 She wasn't invited to the party.
6 We were taken to the hospital.
7 They weren't given any information.
8 Was the missing child found?
9 Were you disturbed in the night?

13 1 was 2 Did 3 were 4 had 5 Was
6 were 7 had 8 was 9 had 10 were

14 3 I got up late this morning, but fortunately I just managed to catch the bus.
4 Actually, my name's John/My name's John, actually, but don't worry.
5 In the middle of the picnic, it suddenly began to rain./Suddenly, in the middle of the picnic, it began to rain.
6 I only saw Mary at the party. I didn't see anyone else.
7 I only gave a present to John, not to anyone else.

8 Jane and I have always been friends. We went to school together. We were even born in the same hospital.

9 A I didn't like it.
B I didn't like it, either.

10 A I like it.
B I like it, too.

11 Everybody in our family really loves ice-cream, especially me.

12 The traffic to the airport was so bad that we nearly missed the plane.

13 I'm tall enough to be a policeman, but I haven't got enough qualifications.

15 2 threw, through   3 wore, war   4 warn, worn   5 caught, court   6 blew, blue
7 knew, new   8 saw, sore   9 read, red
10 rode, road

16 2 at, On, on, in, At, on
3 In, in, —, in
4 in, at, at
5 —, On, In, At
6 At, in

UNIT 4

1 1 2 b   3 b   4 a   5 c   6 a   7 b   8 b   9 c
2 2 Why do you often have to travel overseas?
3 Why do you always have to be home before midnight?
4 Why don't you have to get up at 6.30 a.m. any more?
5 Why does your dad usually have to work in the evenings?
6 Why does your wife have to go to hospital every week?
7 Why doesn't your sister have to help with the housework?
8 Why does your husband have to take the children to school every morning?
9 Why do you have to get good marks in your exams?

2 3 has to, doesn't have to   4 had to, didn't have to   5 'll have to   6 having to   7 Did your grandfather have to   8 don't have to
9 will we have to   10 Do we have to

3 1 2 A security officer at an airport
3 A teacher at a school
4 A librarian in a library
5 A flight attendant on a plane
6 A prisoner in a prison
2 Students' own answers

4 1 ⑭ Jill, ⑨ Jack, ① Jill, ③ Jack, ⑦ Jill, ⑫ Jack, ⑥ Jill
2 ⑩ Sam, ② Anna, ⑤ Sam, ④ Anna, ⑪ Sam, ⑬ Anna, ⑧ Sam

5 1 Sample answers
2 You should buy another one.
3 You should try to cut down on coffee.
4 He should start a new hobby.
5 You should have a haircut!

2 2 Should I go to   3 should I order
4 Should I tell him   5 should I take
6 should I say

6 2 I must do my homework tonight. a
I have to do my homework tonight b
3 We must go to Paris sometime. b
We have to go to Paris next week. a
4 I must wear something nice to go clubbing. a
Men have to wear a shirt and tie to go into a posh restaurant. b
5 I must water the plants today. a
You have to water the plants daily. b

7 2 mustn't   3 don't have to   4 mustn't
5 doesn't have to   6 don't have to
7 don't have to   8 mustn't   9 mustn't
10 don't have to

8 2 must, have to   3 must, have to
4 mustn't, don't have to   5 must, have to
6 don't have to, mustn't

9
Noun	Verb
2 ad'vice	ad'vise
3 intro'duction	intro'duce
4 invi'tation	in'vite
5 'meeting	meet
6 relax'ation	re'lax
7 dis'cussion	dis'cuss
8 re'fusal	re'fuse
9 'feeling	feel
10 gift	give
11 bow	bow
12 'prayer	pray
13 in'vention	in'vent
14 choice	choose

Noun	Adjective
15 nation'ality	'national
16 tra'dition	tra'ditional
17 pro'fession	pro'fessional
18 'illness	ill
19 'value	'valuable
20 truth	true
21 'difference	'different
22 'freedom	free
23 'culture	'cultural
24 responsi'bility	re'sponsible
25 ne'cessity	'necessary

10 Ms M   It's Ms Maddox actually.
Ms M   Ms Maureen Maddox.
Ms M   No, in fact, I want to borrow five thousand pounds.
Ms M   No. I want to open a flower shop for my daughter. Don't you think you should read my loan application, Mr Sanders?
Ms M   But you sent me a form last week, and I'm ringing because I have some queries about it.
Ms M   No, I haven't filled in the form. I can't fill it in because I don't understand it. That's why I'm ringing.
Ms M   Not any more. I don't want to ask you questions about anything!! Good bye!

11 2 look at it   3 Don't throw it away
4 Turn it down   5 looking forward to it
6 make it up   7 tried it on   8 Pick it up
9 look after it   10 Give it back

UNIT 5

1 2 'll get   3 'll give
4 're going to have, 'll get
5 will you be, 'll call
6 will win/is going to win, will win/is going to win
7 'll fetch
8 'll give, are you going to do, 'm going to see
9 are you going to start, 'll do, 'll start
10 will it take
11 'll like, are you going to do

2 2 Where are they going?
They're going shopping.
3 Where are they going?
They're going skateboarding.
4 Where's he going?
He's going fishing.
5 Where's she going?
She's going skiing.
6 Where are they going?
They're going sailing.

3 2 'll feel better   3 he'll help   4 won't give me any   5 it'll rain   6 'll get burnt
7 won't like it

4 Sample answers
2 I'll get you some water.
3 I'll answer it for you.
4 I'll lend you some.
5 I'll give you a lift.
6 I'll help you carry them.

5 2 are you inviting   3 're driving
4 're bringing   5 are you getting   6 is delivering   7 is … making   8 are you giving   9 're travelling   10 (we're) staying

6 2 're going   3 's going to rain   4 won't tell   5 'll lend   6 're going to have
7 's being delivered   8 's taking

7 3 anybody/anyone, nobody/no one
4 anybody/anyone
5 somewhere
6 anything
7 somewhere
8 nothing
9 Anywhere
10 everybody/everyone
11 Anything
12 Nobody/No one, nothing
13 Everybody/Everyone
14 anywhere

8 1 **make** up your mind, a decision, a mess, a complaint, sure that, my bed, money, a speech, a profit, a noise, a phone call, friends with, progress
do the shopping, someone a favour, the housework, nothing, my best, exercises, the washing-up

2 1 made up her mind/made her mind up
  2 do exercises 3 do nothing
  4 make a noise 5 doing my best
  6 made a complaint
  7 does the washing-up 8 do me a favour
  9 made a speech 10 made friends with
  11 make a phone call 12 make sure

9 1 2 /e/ 3 /ʊ/ 4 /ʊ/ 5 /ɪ/ 6 /ʌ/ 7 /ɑː/
  2 2 break /eɪ/ 3 won't /əʊ/
    4 wonder /ʌ/ 5 hungry /ʌ/
    6 breath /e/ 7 wooden /ʊ/
    8 work /ɜː/ 9 ferry /e/
  3 1 beach 2 exploring 3 churches
    4 museums 5 restaurants 6 favourite
    7 delicious 8 different 9 sculptures
    10 jewellery

10 1 in, in, in
  2 in, on, in, in, on, on, at, in, on
  3 B At C At D In E At F In G At
    H On

UNIT 6

1 1 Sample answers
  1 I like working in small groups most.
  2 I like working with a partner.
  3 I'd like to have less homework.
  4 It's very nice; it's not very big, but there are some plants and it's light and comfortable.
  5 They're really nice!
  6 It's not very good, but it's getting better.
  7 I'd like to speak more in class, and write more at home.
  2 3 What's your job like?
    4 Who do you look like in your family?
    5 What did you look like as a child?
    6 Would you like coffee or tea?
    7 Do you like tennis?
    8 Would you like to go to the cinema?
    9 What's your house like?
    10 How are your parents?
  3 1 was it like 2 what was that like
    3 what were they like
    4 What do they look like
    5 What was that like?
    6 did you like 7 would you like

2 1 2 i 3 d 4 a 5 b 6 h 7 f 8 c 9 g
  2 2 What would you like to do tonight?
    3 Where would you like to go on holiday?
    4 Would you like an ice-cream?
    5 What sort of music do you like listening to?
    6 Do you like swimming?
    7 Would you like to go swimming?
    8 Would you like to be a teacher?

3 2 like 3 as 4 like 5 like 6 like 7 like
  8 as 9 like 10 like 11 as, as 12 like
  13 as 14 like

4 1 you to be 2 smoking 3 to help
  4 to tell 5 to going 6 have 7 to go
  8 watching

5 2 Watching 3 mending 4 Finding
  5 waking up 6 walking 7 helping
  8 Living 9 Giving up 10 working

6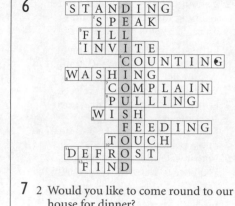

S T A N D I N G
S P E A K
F I L L
I N V I T E
C O U N T I N G
W A S H I N G
C O M P L A I N
P U L L I N G
W I S H
F E E D I N G
T O U C H
D E F R O S T
F I N D

7 2 Would you like to come round to our house for dinner?
  3 I like it when you laugh at my jokes.
  4 ✓ 5 ✓ 6 ✓
  7 Alan thinks it's too expensive, and I agree.
  8 She thinks she's right, but I don't agree.
  9 ✓ 10 ✓
  11 She thought we should go, and I agreed.
  12 They agreed to talk about it again tomorrow.

8 1 2 a married person a return ticket
    3 a dark colour a heavy suitcase
    4 an easy test a soft pillow
    5 a long film a tall man
    6 a mild curry a cold drink
    7 fair hair a light room
  2 3 a well-off/wealthy woman
    4 an amusing story
    5 a messy room
    6 correct information
    7 nice/kind/helpful people
    8 a stupid/foolish person
    9 an intelligent person
    10 a great/brilliant/fantastic/an excellent idea
    11 dreadful/terrible news
    12 horrible/revolting food

9 2 Anna's got long blonde hair.
  3 Do you want a single ticket?
  4 Does Liz like red wine?
  5 Did he say that the film was boring?
  6 Do Jane and Paul like going for walks?
  7 Would you like a hot drink?
  8 Have you got a headache?
  9 I liked school when I was a child.

10 1 2 j 3 g 4 k 5 a 6 i 7 b 8 l 9 h
    10 c 11 f 12 e
  2 2 find out 3 fill it in 4 sort it all out
    5 put it out 6 try out 7 try these jeans on 8 work out 9 clear everything up 10 Take them back

UNIT 7

1 1 c has she made d did she make
    e did he make f has he made
    g has he painted h did he paint
  2 2 g 3 a 4 f 5 d 6 e 7 b 8 h
  3 2 did he move 3 did she write
    4 was he when he

2 1 was born 2 has been 3 studied
  4 has travelled 5 went 6 was painted

7 has also designed 8 has lived
  9 has never 10 lives

3 1 B We've been on holiday.
    A Where did you go?
    B We went to Spain.
    A When did you get back?
    B Last night. The plane landed at 6.00 in the evening.
  2 A What have you done to your finger?
    B I've cut/I cut myself.
    A How did you do that?
    B I was cooking and the knife slipped.
    A Have you put anything on it?
    B No. It's not that bad.

4 1 gone 2 been 3 been 4 gone 5 been
  6 been 7 gone

5 1

	Past Simple	Present Perfect
3	✓	✗
4	✓	✗
5	✓	✗
6	✓	✓
7	✓	✓
8	✗	✓
9	✗	✓
10	✓	✓

  2 1 I've just heard about your accident.
    2 Have you had breakfast yet?
    3 I've already finished my exams.
    4 Have you ever been to Thailand?
    5 I haven't seen that film yet.
  3 1 I haven't finished yet.
    2 No, thanks. I've just had one.
    3 I'm sorry. He's just gone out.
    4 Has it/the match started yet?
    5 I haven't done my homework yet.
    6 I've already fed her.

6 Students' own answers.

7 1 How long have you known the teacher?
  2 This is the first time I've eaten Thai food.
  3 What did you do last night?
  4 I studied/I've been studying English for four years.
  5 When did you get your hair cut?
  6 I saw Peter yesterday.

8 1 I **Have** you **been** to university?
    S Yes, I have. I **went** to Bristol University from 1995 to 1998.
    I What subjects **did you study**?
    S **Music** and **Sociology**.
    I **Do you speak** any languages?
    S Yes, I do. I **speak Spanish** fluently.
    I **Have you** ever **lived** in Spain?
    S Yes, I **have**. I **lived** and **worked** in Barcelona for a year.
    I What kind of work **did** you **do** there?
    S I **was/worked as an English assistant in a junior school**.
    I What **are you doing** now?
    S **I'm a music therapist at a children's hospital** near Exeter.
    I How long **have you been working** there?
    S Since **April 1998**.
  2 1 lives 2 studied 3 learned, lived 4 has worked/has been working 5 likes
    6 worked

9 2 've applied   3 have you been injured
4 has just lost   5 has passed
6 has been given   7 has risen
8 has been called   9 haven't been offered
10 have you saved

10 1 1 dropped   2 were lost   3 rang
4 has been found   5 was discovered
6 have been put   7 have … announced
8 have been stolen   9 have been valued
10 were taken   11 did not go off   12 was
not discovered   13 have … been found
2 2 When was his wallet discovered?
3 What has been stolen from the
Museum of Modern Art?
4 Have the paintings been valued by
experts?
5 When do police believe that they were
taken?
6 Have any clues been found?

11 1 Students' own answers.
2 Students use their dictionaries.

12
A	B	C
business	degree	applicant
fluent	Japan	editor
foreign	resign	interesting
	career	journalist

D	E	F
behaviour	Argentina	experience
discover	absolutely	interpreter
pollution	competition	political
	publication	

13 2 on   3 out of   4 for   5 on   6 between
7 about   8 with   9 for   10 on   11 in
12 of

UNIT 8

1 1 If you go to Paris, you must go to the
top of the Eiffel Tower. The views are
fantastic.
2 If we can afford it, we'll buy a new car
soon. The one we have now is very
unreliable.
3 If I don't hear from you today, I'll phone
you tomorrow. I need to talk to you
about something.
4 If the music is too loud, you can turn
down the radio. I don't mind.
5 If we don't leave soon, we'll be late for
school. It'll be the second time this week.
6 If there's nothing interesting in the
window, go inside the shop. You might
find something you like.
7 If she has to work late, she'll phone you
from the office. She might not be home
until 9.00.
8 If Daniel rings, tell him I never want to
see him again. He really hurt my feelings.

2 Shopping   7 Lisa,   2 Tom,   3 Lisa,
5 Tom,   13 Lisa,   9 Tom,   10 Lisa,   15 Tom

Barbeque   8 Pete,   14 Jody,   1 Pete,   11
Jody,   6 Pete,   16 Jody

3 Sample answers
2 If you can't get to sleep, get up and
make yourself some hot chocolate.

3 If you get sunburned, put some cream
on and stay out of the sun.
4 If you want to stop smoking, throw all
your cigarettes away!
5 If you have a problem at school, tell a
teacher.
6 If you can't wake up in the mornings,
get two alarm clocks!

4 1 2 I want to finish my work before we go
out.
3 She's going to look after the cat while
I'm away on holiday.
4 I'll email you as soon as I arrive.
5 We'll find a hotel when we arrive in
Paris.
6 She won't speak to him until he says
sorry.
7 Drink your coffee before it gets cold.
8 Don't cross the road until you see the
green man.
9 I'll give you a ring after we get back
from holiday.
10 Are you going to stay with Paola while
you're in Italy?
2 1 When   2 if   3 after   4 As soon as
5 before   6 until   7 As soon as   8 If
9 until   10 while   11 after   12 when
13 If

5 2 If I didn't have a headache, I'd go
swimming.
3 If I knew the answer, I'd tell you.
4 If we had any money, we'd have a
holiday this year.
5 If I had some spare time, I'd learn Russian.
6 If we had a big house, we could/we'd be
able to invite friends to stay.
7 If there were some eggs, I would make a
cake.
8 If I were cleverer, I'd be a doctor.
9 If I had a mobile, you could call me.
10 He could win the lottery if he bought a
ticket.
11 If Francis didn't work so hard, he would
have time to spend with his family.
12 If we didn't have/hadn't got three
children, we'd take a year off and travel
the world.

6 1 rains, won't be able   2 pass, 'll post
3 had, 'd take up   4 were/was, could
5 don't have, will go
6 had, would … disappear
7 need, 'll come   8 could, would open
9 are, will … buy   10 were, 'd go

7 2 If I could go anywhere in the world, I'd
go to Fiji.
3 If I see Jane, I'll tell her to phone you.
4 If I had lots of money, I'd buy an
aeroplane.
5 When I go back to university, I'll email
you.
6 If you knew my brother, you'd know
what I mean!
7 If you came from my town, you would
recognize the street names.
8 If you aren't careful, you'll lose your bag.

8 Students' own answers

9 1 **Noun**
currency, safe, accountant, waste, win,
millionaire, economy, cash machine,
credit card, loan, will, windfall, salary,
bet, savings, coins, spending spree,
cashier, wages, cheque, fortune
Verb
waste, win, earn, save, loan, will, bet, invest
Adjective
wealthy, safe, broke, bankrupt,
economic, penniless, economical
2 2 broke   3 economic   4 invested
5 currency   6 an accountant   7 cash
machine   8 bet   9 wealthy
10 salary is   11 will

10
A /ʊ/	B /uː/	C /ʌ/
cooks	spoon	blood
wooden	pool	flooded
look	pools	
football	foolishly	
booked	room	
woollen	cool	
stood	stool	
	roof	

11 1 2 sour   3 country   4 though   5 cough
6 mouse   7 doubt   8 though
2 1 thought, counts   2 enormous, mouse
3 doubt, furious   4 ought, cough
5 trouble, neighbours

12 2 work out   3 Hang on   4 Hang on!
5 going on   6 Go on   7 put out
8 put out   9 get over   10 get over
11 make it up   12 make up

UNIT 9

1 2 h   3 d   4 j   5 g   6 i   7 c   8 b   9 f   10 a

2 1 2 He must be ill.
3 He might be in the coffee bar.
4 He could have a doctor's
appointment.
5 He may be stuck in a traffic jam.
6 His bus might be late.
7 He must want to miss the test.
2 Sample answers
2 He can't be ill because he phoned me
this morning.
3 He can't be in the coffee bar because
it isn't open yet.
4 He can't have a doctor's appointment
because the surgery is closed now.
5 He can't be stuck in a traffic jam
because the rush hour is over now.
6 His bus can't be late because they go
every few minutes from his street.
7 He can't want to miss the test, because
he always gets the best mark!

3 2 be listening, be having
3 be sitting
4 be reading
5 be taking
6 be holding, be going
7 be digging, be mending

4 Sample answers
2 He must have had an accident. He
might have been skydiving.

3 She might have been for a long walk.
   She may have got sore feet.
4 He must be frightened. He might have
   got lost.
5 They might have had an argument.
   They may be bored.
6 They might have won the lottery. They
   must have received some good news.

5 2 You can't have worked hard for your
     exams.
   3 They could have gone to the station.
   4 I might have left my mobile in the
     Internet café.
   5 He can't have bought another new car.
   6 He must have been on a diet.
   7 They could have got married in secret.
   8 He may have called while we were out.

6 Possible answers
   2 2 ✗ They can't have been husband and
       wife.
       ✓ They definitely lived together.
     3 ✓ They must have been together for a
       long time.
       ✗ They can't have been together for a
       long time.
     4 ✗ He might be glad she's gone.
       ✓ He must be missing her very much.
     5 ✓ The house must seem very quiet.
       ? He might have pets to keep him
       company.
     6 ? He must have done something to
       upset her.
       ✓ She has definitely done something
       to upset him.
     7 ✗ He can't be using the bathroom
       much.
       ✓ He might be trying to avoid using
       the bathroom.
     8 ✓ She must have spent a lot of time in
       the bathroom.
       ✓ The bathroom might have been her
       favourite room.
     9 ✓ He might be sleeping downstairs.
       ? He can't be sleeping in their old
       bedroom.

7 1 | **Adjective** | **Noun** |
   |---|---|
   | shy | shyness |
   | optimistic | optimism |
   | reliable | reliability |
   | ambitious | ambition |
   | lazy | laziness |
   | pessimistic | pessimism |
   | generous | generosity |
   | tidy | tidiness |
   | moody | moodiness |
   | sensitive | sensitivity |

   2 1 moody 2 shyness 3 reliable
     4 ambition 5 optimistic 6 generosity
     7 tidiness 8 laziness

8 1 1 She must have eaten the cheese.
     2 You can't have seen him.
     3 He can't have arrived early.
     4 He might have gone out for a cup of
       coffee.
     5 She might have been angry.
     6 They can't have been in love.
     7 They might have written it down.

8 He must have been to Africa.
2 1 He could have gone abroad.
  2 They might have eaten it all.
  3 She may be arriving this evening.
  4 They must be coming soon.
  5 They can't know him at all.

9 3 Mrs 4 put 5 train 6 a 7 might
   8 can't

10 2 with 3 at 4 to 5 from 6 about
    7 of 8 for 9 to 10 of 11 of 12 for
    13 of 14 of 15 in 16 of 17 about
    18 about 19 for 20 with

UNIT 10

1 1 3 been waiting 4 broken 5 eaten
   6 been running 7 met 8 known
   9 been writing 10 written 11 been
   watching 12 watched

2 2 's had
   3 has moved, 've been looking, haven't
     found
   4 've been shopping, haven't bought
   5 've … heard
   6 have you been doing, 've been working
   7 's been snowing
   8 've been listening, haven't understood
   9 've been working
   10 've been trying, 've lost

2 2 have you been learning (to drive)
     Have you
   3 has he been a teacher
     has he taught in
   4 have you been waiting
   5 people have they
     has she
   6 have you been
     have you
   7 has she been there/to the States
   8 started
   9 has she gone
   10 has she been going there/to France

3 2 b a 3 a b 4 b a 5 a b 6 a b 7 b
   a 8 b a

4 2 comes 3 is coming 4 works 5 has
   worked/has been working 6 has had
   7 had 8 wants 9 is thinking 10 don't
   think 11 to find 12 be working
   13 went 14 woke, was raining 15 is
   taking, has 16 to go 17 be sitting

5 1 When was Richard born?
   2 How long did he study at Cherwell School?
     Until he was eighteen.
   3 How long was he at Bath University?
   4 How long did he go out with Helena?
     For four years.
   5 How long did he work in Madrid?
     For six months.
   6 Where did he meet Heather?
   7 How long has he been working in the
     bookshop?
     Since 1999.
   8 How long has he been the manager?
     Since 2002.
   9 When did he marry Heather?
     On 23 March 2001.

10 How long have they had a house in
   Woodstock?
   Since Richard was 26.
11 How long did Heather live in Australia?
   Until she was 18.
12 How long has she been interested in
   drama?
   Since she was 11.
13 When did she meet Harry?
   While she was working in Hungary.
14 When did she get married for the first
   time?
   In 1996.
15 When was Joanne born?
   On 13 May 1997.
16 How long was Heather married to Harry?
   For two years.
17 How long has she been teaching in the
   school in Oxford?
   Since 1998.
18 When did she meet Richard?
   At Christmas time in 1998.

6 Sample answers
   1 2 thoughtful, thoughtless,
       thoughtlessness
     3 disagree, agreeable, agreement
     4 careful, careless, carelessness
     5 hopeful, hopeless, hopelessness
     6 unconscious, consciousness
     7 inhuman, humanity, inhumanity
     8 successful, unsuccessful
     9 impolite, politeness
     10 helpful, unhelpful, helpless,
        helplessness
     11 misunderstand, understandable,
        understanding
     12 tasteful, tasteless, distaste, distasteful
     13 illegal, legality
     14 illogical, logically
     15 distress, stressful
     16 unpopular, popularity
     17 misuse, disuse, useful, useless
     18 unlike, dislike, likeable, likeness,
        unlikeable

   2 2 hopeless 3 Politeness 4 helpful
     5 successful 6 unlike
     7 misunderstand 8 careful, useless
     9 stress, thoughtless 10 disagreements

7 1 1 clear, beer 2 where, bear 3 stay,
       weigh 4 know, phone 5 shy, high
       6 enjoy, noise 7 now, aloud 8 sure, poor
   2 1 plane, south, Spain
     2 boy, coat, enjoyed
     3 known, nearly, five
     4 wearing, rose, hair
     5 smoke, pipes, days
     6 likes, ride, motorbike

8 1 at 2 for, from, to 3 during, at 4 in, on
   5 For 6 Until 7 in 8 since 9 at 10 At

UNIT 11

1 1 2 Do 3 Did 4 Was 5 Has 6 Have
   7 Does 8 Did

   2 Correct answers
     1 Yes, it is. 2 Yes, they do. 3 Yes, they
     did. 4 No, he wasn't. Theodore
     Roosevelt was. 5 No, there hasn't.

6 Yes, the Olympic Games have been held in London twice, in 1908 and 1948
7 No, it doesn't. It has a prime minister.
8 Yes, he did.

2 1 2 What 3 Where 4 Who 5 What
6 Who 7 When 8 Which
2 Correct answers
1 Gibraltar, Spain, France, Monaco, Italy, Slovenia, Croatia, Serbia and Montenegro, Albania, Greece, Turkey, Cyprus, Syria, Israel, Lebanon, Egypt, Libya, Malta, Tunisia, Algeria, Morocco
2 Earthquakes 3 Greek 4 Yuri Gagarin
5 National Aeronautics and Space Administration
6 Grace Kelly 7 1994 8 Jamaica

3 2 what time it is/what the time is
3 where you put them
4 what I'm going to give him/what to give him yet.
5 whether I posted it/your letter or not.
6 whose coat it is
7 if I'm going (on the rollercoaster).
8 who … is
9 how much they/Frankie's trainers cost.
10 what his job is.

4 2 We don't know exactly how old he is.
3 I wonder how he's going to celebrate his birthday.
4 Nobody knows how he managed to get out.
5 I wonder who helped him to escape.
6 I didn't know she'd been married so many times.
7 I wonder if this will be the last time.
8 I'd like to know what the score was.
9 The headline doesn't say who they were playing against.
10 I wonder how he graduated so quickly.
11 I wonder if he is a good doctor.

5 2 I've no idea how many have French ancestry.
3 Do you know what the official language is?
4 I'm not sure exactly where Montreal is situated.
5 I haven't a clue who discovered Montreal.
6 I wonder what the buildings are like.
7 Could you tell me how long winter lasts?
8 Do you know why they have built an underground city?
9 I don't know if there are any film or jazz festivals.
10 Have you any idea where 'poutine' is sold?

6 1 2 Who is he waiting for?
3 Who does she work for?
4 What are you talking about?
5 Who did you stay with?
6 Who does that bike belong to?
7 Who is the letter from?
8 What did he die of?
9 What are you worried about?
10 Who are you writing to?
11 What are you staring at?
2 2 What about? 3 Where to? 4 What for? 5 Who with? 6 What about? 7 What about? 8 What for? 9 What about? 10 What with?

7 2 do you 3 aren't you 4 didn't we
5 isn't it 6 can you 7 will you 8 do we
9 have you 10 did they

8 1 2 You don't want to go to the party, do you?
3 You ate too much, didn't you?
4 That dress is lovely, isn't it?
5 That concert was wonderful, wasn't it?
6 You aren't enjoying the film, are you?
2 2 Sue, you couldn't lend me five pounds, could you?
3 Nuria, you don't know where my sunglasses are, do you?
4 Ravi, you haven't got a red pen, have you?
5 Sarah, you haven't seen Bill, have you?
6 Excuse me, you haven't got change for a twenty-euro note, have you?
3 Exercise 1: the question tags go down. Exercise 2: the question tags go up.

9 1 2 aren't they? aren't we?
3 are you? can't I? aren't you?
4 isn't it? doesn't he? would you?

10 'When did the world begin and how?'
I asked a lamb, a goat, a cow.
'What's it all about and why?'
I asked a pig as he went by.
'Where will the whole thing end, and when?'
I asked a duck, a goose, a hen.
And I copied all their answers too,
A quack, a baa, an oink, a moo.
Animal noises: quack (duck), baa (lamb/goat), oink (pig), moo (cow)

11 1 roared 2 whisper 3 screamed
4 groaning 5 banged 6 smashed
7 scratched 8 whistling

12 1 going on 2 set off 3 came across
4 put up with 5 takes up 6 keep on
7 pick you up 8 let me down 9 fallen out with 10 Come on

UNIT 12

1 Tom It's your fault that we went to Mexico. The holiday cost a fortune and it was the worst I've ever had.

Karen There's nothing wrong with Mexico – it's very beautiful. The travel agency are to blame. Their brochure promised all kinds of things about the hotel. And they were all lies. You've no right to blame me.

Tom I'm sorry, Karen. I know it's not really your fault. I'll go to the travel agent first thing in the morning and I'll tell them everything that went wrong.

Karen I'll come too because I'm going to ask for our money back or another holiday.

2 2 had 3 led 4 were 5 would have

3 1 2 She said she was going to Berlin soon.
3 I thought the film would be interesting.
4 She said she couldn't help me because she had too much to do.

5 I was told that Daniel had bought the tickets.
6 She said she thought it was a stupid idea and it wouldn't work.
7 The tour guide explained that the banks were closed on Saturdays.
8 He complained that they'd had terrible weather on holiday.
9 They told me they'd never been to Brazil.
2 2 She asked me if I wanted to go out for a walk.
3 They wondered why she was crying.
4 He asked me if he could borrow my car.
5 The customs officer asked me where I'd come from.
6 She wanted to know how long I was going to be at the gym.
7 Trudi wondered if I'd bought any milk.
8 She asked us if we'd be back early.
9 She asked me when I had to go to work.
3 2 And why do you need it?
3 What do you do?
4 And how much do you earn?
5 Are you married?
6 Have you got any children?
7 How long have you lived there?
8 When would you like the money?
4 2 Then she wanted to know why he needed it.
3 She needed to know what he did.
4 He had to tell her how much he earned.
5 Then she asked if he was married.
6 For some reason, she wanted to know if he had any children.
7 She asked him how long he had lived in his flat.
8 Finally, she wondered when he would like the money.

4 2 He asked Sue if she could cook dinner.
3 The teacher told the class to hand in their homework on Monday.
4 My wife reminded me to post the letter.
5 Marta invited Paul to have dinner with them.
6 The judge ordered Edward Fox to pay a fine of £200.
7 Flora persuaded Emily to buy the black shoes.
8 Marco encouraged Anthony to sing professionally.
9 She begged me not to tell her father.

5 2 He asked her not to go.
3 He told Debra he was going to bed.
4 Jeremy asked his father how much he earned.
5 The teacher told the class to turn to page 34.
6 The secretary asked Miss Fulton to call back later.
7 The teacher told the class they did very well in the test.
8 The police officer told the children not to run across the road.
9 Pam asked Roy if he was going to the concert.
10 Harry told his daughters it was time to get up.

6 2 Jo agreed to lend Matt ten Euros.
3 Harry admitted that he had broken the camera.
4 Timmy denied that he had pulled her hair.
5 The professor boasted that he could speak eleven languages perfectly.
6 Jessica's dad promised to buy her a pizza if she finished all her homework.
7 Patrick complained that there was a fly in his salad.
8 Sarah refused to marry Adrian because she didn't love him.
9 Amanda offered to cook supper for her and Duncan.

7 2 told   3 asked   4 said   5 asked
6 explained   7 tell   8 speak
9 replied/said   10 do you ask   11 tell
12 speak/talk   13 said   14 talk   15 said

8 1 2 birthday   3 born   4 birth   5 BIRTH
6 birth   7 birthday
2 2 death   3 died   4 die   5 dead, die
6 dying   7 death   8 dead   9 die, die
3 2 married   3 been married   4 marry
5 wedding   6 got married   7 get married

9 **A** honeymoon, actually, terrible, opposite, counsellor, funeral
B cancelled, marriage, colleague
C forever, announcement, reception, reminded
D complained, invite, engaged, bouquet, accused

10 1 2 would   3 had   4 had   5 would   6 would
2 1 She said that she'd seen him.(had)
2 She said that she'd see him soon.(would)
3 He told her he'd loved her for a long time.(had)
4 He told her he'd love her forever.(would)

11 2 down on   3 on with   4 away from
5 on with   6 up with   7 back on
8 forward to   9 out of

REVISION

Tenses

1 2 h   3 g   4 c   5 a   6 e   7 f   8 b

2 2 Has Madonna been in a film?
3 I'm not doing a French exercise.
4 He wasn't president in 1984.
5 They haven't got any children.
6 Where are you going after the lesson?
7 What does 'perform' mean?
8 Did you have a sandwich for lunch?
9 Do you enjoy learning English?

Present tenses

1 2 am not eating   3 fly   4 go   5 is she doing   6 don't visit   7 Do … fix   8 Are
9 's snowing   10 're having   11 don't live … live   12 works … travels
13 are studying   14 is going
2 2 a   3 b   4 a   5 a   6 a   7 a
3 2 are kept   3 is being helped   4 are invited   5 am paid   6 are being taken
7 are being built   8 are thrown

Past tenses

1 1B waited … took
2A doesn't look
2B isn't … phoned … was sleeping
3A Did … watch
3B saw … was doing
4A Were … looking
4B wanted
5A started … was living
5B didn't know

2 2 didn't ring … had forgotten
3 hadn't passed … drove
4 got … remembered … had left
5 didn't know … had walked
6 heard … had applied
7 went … had never travelled
8 didn't enjoy… had seen
9 didn't know … had met
10 had been … had

3 1 had never met   2 owned   3 stood
4 were   5 knew   6 seemed   7 were walking   8 noticed   9 was   10 decided
11 was   12 were walking   13 could hear
14 was crying   15 went   16 found
17 was lying   18 had fallen   19 had managed   20 was

4 2 was painted   3 was sent   4 were written
5 was not brought   6 were helped

Modals 1

1 2 2 Can I use his car?
3 She/He can use his car.
3 1 I shouldn't write to them.
2 Should I write to them?
3 He/She should write to them.
4 1 I don't have to phone them.
2 Must I phone them?
3 She/He must phone them.

2 2 b   3 f   4 d   5 a   6 e

Future forms

1 2 Greg will help you to move the computer.
3 Don't ask Al, he won't help you.
4 Kate is catching the train at 3.30 this afternoon.
5 They're not going to visit us next summer.
6 Are you going to meet them at the airport?

2 2 b   3 a   4 b   5 a   6 a   7 a   8 b

3 B Are you going   A am applying
B I'm having   A I'll buy
B I'm getting   A I'll see

Questions with *like*

2 a   3 b   4 a   5 b   6 b

Verb patterns

2 to turn   3 spending   4 to train
5 to wait   6 working   7 to go
8 speaking   9 waiting   10 to arrive

Present Perfect

1 A Have … started
A Have … found
B haven't … 've seen
A Have … visited
B have … 've been … haven't been
A Has … started
B has

2 2 didn't receive   3 learnt   4 worked
5 went   6 has lived   7 have been
8 Have … won   9 hasn't spoken
10 hasn't been

3 2 has sunk   3 have caused   4 have left
5 have been put   6 has been arrested   7 has been awarded

Conditionals

1 2 If you run, you'll catch the train.
3 I won't ring you, unless I'm late.
4 If it's sunny, we'll go to the beach.
5 I won't go to the football match if Beckham isn't playing.
6 She will be very unhappy if he doesn't ring her.

2 (Answers will vary.)

3 2 are   3 forgot   4 'll tell   5 'd take
6 wouldn't run   7 is   8 'll be   9 had

Modals 2

2 c   3 g   4 a   5 b   6 i   7 f   8 d   9 e

Present Perfect Simple or Continuous?

1 2 's been raining   3 I've cleaned   4 've cooked   5 's bought   6 've been cleaning … 've done   7 has been sleeping
8 have been looking

2 2 looking … hasn't   3 living … decided
4 working   5 broken   6 seen … gone
7 sitting … written   8 trying … got
9 finished … read   10 heard … won/lost

Indirect questions

1 (Answers will vary.)

2 2 where he lives   3 he arrived?   4 he has been   5 I was doing   6 he has put
7 he thinks   8 you are ready

Question tags

2 is it?   3 have you?   4 isn't he?   5 did I?
6 haven't you?   7 wasn't it?   8 will you?   9 doesn't he?   10 had he?

Reported speech

1 2 had some champagne in the fridge
3 had seen him yesterday
4 he didn't know the answer
5 had lived in London a long time ago
6 hadn't known him long
7 what his girlfriend's name was
8 what school she had been to
9 if he'd seen the news
10 where her friend worked
11 how long they were staying
12 what time it began

2 2 advised   3 refused   4 ordered   5 asked
6 reminded   7 told